ex libris
Eugène J. Boutin, ptre.

HEARTBREAK   EARTH

HEARTBREAK
EARTH

by

A CARMELITE NUN
Author of " Our Eternal Vocation "
" World Without End ", " Each Hour Remains "

THE NEWMAN PRESS

Westminster, Maryland

1953

Nihil obstat: EDUARDUS MAHONEY, S.T.D.
CENSOR DEPUTATUS.

Imprimatur: E. MORROGH BERNARD
VIC. GEN.

Westmonasterii, die 30a Septembris, 1952

Library of Congress Catalog Card Number: 53-5589

PRINTED IN THE UNITED STATES OF AMERICA

TO

MONSIGNOR

CONTENTS

THE OVERTURE

THE train drew out of the station of Civita Vecchia and began to cross the plain which lay between it and Rome. The setting sun was uncomfortably hot and the passengers weary; in the far distance the edges of the hills cut the horizon into jagged patterns against the marvel of the sky. Blue, pink, green and saffron, it rose tier upon tier above the violet of the evening mist which already lay over the quiet fields. The passengers, American and English, chatted desultorily with the easy friendliness of passing travelling-companions. For no particular reason the conversation turned upon religious orders, then upon nuns, and finally, following up the casual remark of a priest in one of the corner seats, upon enclosed religious life.

"Bats," pronounced a young married woman, kindly but comprehensively.

A girl in the opposite corner raised her eyes for a moment from her book, then dropped them again. They were rather remarkable eyes, the priest thought, and wondered why she was coming to Rome. The conversation continued to buzz around him.

"Well, if they don't do any good at least they don't do any harm," said another woman broadmindedly, "after all there is no accounting for tastes."

"Anyone who is not pulling her weight in the present-day world is doing harm," said the heavy aunt with the waterproof, abruptly casting her shadow over the assembled company and the whole discussion. "No one should be allowed to evade his or her responsibilities towards the human race in general and . . ."

"Well, not everyone wants to get married," put in the young man from Scotland, "and the others must do something."

"Careers! " cried the shorthand-typist on the opposite seat, who had private but far-reaching designs on political life. "What's wrong with a career?"

"Exactly! " said the heavy aunt, glaring at the young man from over the Border, "that's what I said." It wasn't, but nobody liked to tell her so.

"Nothing that I know of," he replied amiably, "if you can get one." He passed to the defensive as most people did with the heavy aunt. "Not so many women as all that have them, after all."

"Don't you think the enclosed religious life *is* a career?" asked the priest suddenly, turning from the window. "What else would you call it?" The passengers glanced at each other, nonplussed. When it came to the point nobody seemed to want to call it anything in particular—anyway not to a priest. The girl in the corner smiled slightly and went on reading. "What do *you* think?" he suggested, but before she had time to reply the psychological lecturer further up the carriage cut in.

"Result of a complex," he said authoritatively, "inferiority complex causing an inhibition." The listeners were visibly impressed.

"I heard a nice story about complexes the other day," remarked the girl in the corner in her pleasant English drawl. "Like me to tell it you? At the end of his patient's first visit the psychiatrist rose to his feet. 'This isn't a case of a complex,' he said, 'you *are* inferior.'" She went on reading. One of the Americans sniggered, then turned it into a cough.

The train ran into the outskirts of Rome and several of the passengers stood up and began to collect their small luggage. The priest leaned forward under cover of the momentary bustle.

"You are going to enter an enclosed order yourself?" he said in a low voice.

She looked at him calmly. "Oh, yes," she said.

"Here?"

"Oh, no. I've only come to say good-bye."

He nodded. The bustle still obligingly drowned their voices. "Well, I live here," he explained. "Will you sometimes pray for me?"

"Oh, yes."

The train came to a stop alongside the platform and without waiting she got out first. He jumped down beside her.

"I'll say a Mass for you to-morrow morning," he promised, speaking low, then turned at the sound of the voice of a friend who had come to meet him. When he looked back she had gone. He lifted his head to the fresh air and drew in a deep breath.

"It is good to be home," he said with a smile, "surely it is very good to be home." He wondered inconsequently where she was going to stay. "Nice eyes," he commented inwardly, "but she had not much to say. 'Oh, yes,' 'oh, no,' it never got further than that." He and his friend went out of the station together towards the waiting motor.

"Well, Our Lady didn't say much either," he added finally to himself. The car turned down the hill towards the Via Venito; he thought he had never seen the familiar streets look so gay and so enchanting. A twelve foot wall . . . he wondered what it would feel like . . .

a streak of sunshine sometimes he supposed, but never again. . . . He turned his face up to meet the now cool breeze. Well, he would say that Mass for her to-morrow morning anyway, and pray that she would stick it. He reflected a moment on those almost tantalizingly distant eyes and the cool, pleasant voice. Yes, on the whole he felt sure she would stick it. No need to worry. Still, he would say that Mass.

CHAPTER I

THE SPIRITUAL WAR
OF THE TWENTIETH CENTURY

WE live in an age of battles. In whichever direction we turn, our eyes meet signs of potential war, our ears are assailed by rumours and threats of war; uneasily the world crouches and waits, listening for the first signal which may hurl civilization into its final disaster.

War, and the possibility of war, is the portion of this generation. The fact, however unwelcome, has to be accepted, and whatever else we may fight, we are given no opportunity to fight that. It may indeed yet be averted by God's grace, but it is with the Christians of the world that it rests whether or not it shall be averted, and in the meantime it is useless to deny that the dread of it hangs over many people day and night.

This is the Christian's opportunity. A war for God, a battle for civilization, a fight to the last for ethical values and all that makes life beautiful and worth while: let us take up the challenge as individual Christians, and attack on the spiritual plane without waiting to be further attacked on any other. If, in spite of us, it should ever come again to a battle with bombs and physical death—come it must; but at least there need be no spiritual death, and the surest way to avert even material war, is to fight for God with our souls, with our minds, and with all the love in our hearts, here, now, and wherever we go.

In the days of thirty or forty years ago, we are told,

13

young people longed for adventure; they set out to seek their fortune in a world all too dull for their taste and spirit. To-day, by a whimsical inversion of fortune's wheel, the adventure becomes the search for peace; indeed, the treasure island of our fancy might well present itself as the sunlit island where nothing ever happened. The fact is that although all young things are eager for adventure, it is adventure which leads somewhere, which ends in love and glory. The world's proposed adventure of bombs which ends in the destruction of all the actors, including ourselves, is distinctly less alluring, if only for the simple reason that we should not be there to see the *grand finale*. An adventure which ends without us is a poor adventure indeed when we are young and full of life.

Yet the world still holds the kind of enterprise for which the spirit longs: the romantic quest which leads somewhere definite. The way to it is simple. Let us go out in search of God; let us fight for Him, join in battles for Him, bring others to swell the great crusade to be won for Him. We shall have all the adventure we want *en route*, with eternal and infinite love waiting for us at the end, and the glory of God to throw its light over all our days and all our hereafter. The little candle of our own glory, when it goes out, will go without even a wink of extinction and without anybody noticing it, least of all ourselves, for the splendour of God's light is an overwhelming splendour.

This is a war as surely as those other wars which the civilization of the world is so desperately trying to avert; but it is a war of intellects; of religions, of philosophies, of tendencies. In the eyes of many it is the most deadly and sinister form of war, but there is at least this to be said for it: it is a type of war in which Christians can meet and fight their opponents on equal ground. The weapons of one side are, roughly speaking, the weapons of the other: books, the human voice, the wireless, example, life itself.

It is true that the enemy can and does use underground methods of spreading his doctrines which would be distasteful to us, but the very magnificence of the straightforward presentation of truth, the magnanimity of the Christian crusade, are as good weapons as the mole-like activity, the hidden cell-formations, and the insidious whispering campaigns of our opponents. And those opponents are not only the Communists. There are many strange philosophies abroad these days, each one more pagan than the last. Still, taking it all in all, we find ourselves pitting a religion against a religion, an ideal against an ideal, a way of life against a way of life. They can all be summed up as the devil against God, a matter not of the flesh but of the spirit.

With material war, on the contrary, the Christian will always find himself at a disadvantage. Christian nations must of course fight if they are attacked, and fight they will; nevertheless, with the scientifically barbarous weapons of the modern world, they must inevitably be at a disadvantage, not because of any inferiority of actual arms, for our science is as good as theirs; not necessarily because of a numerical disadvantage, since oceans can be crossed in a day and the forces of the West pooled in one enormous camp; but a disadvantage of principle and culture. The higher the principle, the greater the culture, the greater that disadvantage. Thank God, there will always be reluctance on the part of civilized countries to use such weapons as germs, gas, atom and hydrogen bombs, no matter how completely they may possess the secrets; to resort to the use, in short, of those forces of which the use belongs properly to God.

The inevitable hesitations of such reluctance are our

great handicap in modern war, but that handicap does not exist when it comes to religious and ideological war. Subtle, insidious, dangerous as such war may be, it is still of the kind into which we may enter without misgiving, with genuine love of God and of the neighbour in our hearts, and without fear of the result. If we fight firmly and fairly, that result will be according to the will of God in whom we trust, and we need ask no further assurance.

As regards our personal feelings in relation to the battle, we may as well put them entirely on one side. We do not get ready to fight because we want to, but because we ought to. A thing may be overwhelmingly worth while spiritually, but it may not *feel* particularly worth while to our emotions; for we can have the frozen fact of endeavour and achievement without any pleasure in the achievement itself. If there is no sensation of satisfaction in what has to be done, then there will probably be no great sensation of success either, and we shall unconsciously minimize the results to ourselves. It is as well not to confuse the two, the fact and the sensation, particularly in the case of spiritual efforts where, the efforts being made for God, and sometimes only known to God, the feeling of success may often be practically nil. Our pleasure in achievement, ordinarily speaking, arises almost exclusively from human contacts: appreciation, sympathy, praise: but we shall be conscious of none of these when it comes to the affairs of God, and of efforts made solely for His glory.

In spite of this the solid fact of success will remain—if the success *be* a solid fact—no matter how bored, how incredulous, how cold we may feel about it. And that is the thing which gives God honour, and not our feelings. So let us continue undaunted on our chilly way.

Speaking of the spiritual battle only, this can no longer

be averted, for it is already joined, with quite a distressingly large number of the combatants still half asleep. For this, as we said, is total war, and in total war every human being becomes a combatant, whether he will or no. In the second world war, the quietest citizen woke suddenly to find himself the unsuspecting target of bombs; if he wanted to save his life he had to get up and do it; and in this other war, in which you and I have been living for some time, we are the constant targets of every form of ideological weapon known to man. Still drowsy with the fancies and the dreams of night, we must wake to reality at last; to the reality that it is the cities of our souls which have been bombed while we slept; that it is our beliefs, our ideals, our not too clearly held principles which are in mortal danger, if indeed we do not wake to find them already crumbled into dust.

War is in the air and we fight all day, are open to attack all day, wherever we go and with every breath we draw. We fight with each word which we speak, with our smiles, with our laughter; we fight with the pen which we take up to write the simplest letter; with the paper or book which we read and which we lend; with the matters which we will not discuss as well as with those which we will. Every stranger we meet, man or woman, is a possible adversary or a possible companion-in-arms. If an adversary, then our tactics are to convert him; but how are we to do that, since we have never met him before, shall never meet him again, and do not even know if he be friend or foe?

The tactics and the weapons of Christians are surely always the same, and have the great advantage that they will serve equally well to confound the adversary or to encourage the fellow-combatant. Let us set out to show the world (which for us may consist of two streets in a village) that we have something worth while for which to

B

fight: Christianity, civilization. Let us behave consistently as Christians and as civilized persons in an age when the world has gone pagan, and the general effect is of an all-pervading return to the primitive.

The suggestion is so simple that it makes one laugh by its sheer *naïveté*, yet its impact when it is put into practice is quite astonishing. It is rather like the impact of David's stone upon Goliath. For, after all, every Christian is only one of many, and if all Christians behaved as if they were Christians, our battle would already be half won. If, further, all the Christians who know that they ought to be openly so, would come out and take their stand upon the right side—the war would surely be almost over?

We sometimes forget perhaps that the advantages inherent in a person, or in any situation or set of circumstances, can only be used effectively in so far as they are perceived. We can walk amidst material opportunities which would make of someone else either a millionaire or a hero—and walk grumbling that we never get a chance! This we do equally in the spiritual life. We walk among circumstances meant to make saints of us, but we walk blindfold.

Let us take the bandages off our eyes and realize that we are daily engaged in a battle, and that at present it is mainly a war of faith, and intelligence, and spiritual issues, and will only turn into a war of human and material disaster if we fail to use our faith and our intelligence aright. Up to this present era, cultured society everywhere had been on the whole religious; belief was at all events safeguarded. Now religion is no longer necessarily the accepted thing. Just as in material war all the safeguards for the civilian have been abolished, and total war, that is war from all sides at once and upon everybody without restriction, has become the fashion, so, spiritually, the ordinary man and woman, and not only the trained theological expert, is at the mercy of every theory, and the jargon of each new form of philosophy and disbelief.

These matters used to be thrashed out in private among scholars: in universities, in societies, in exclusive lecture-halls and quiet, book-lined studies. They did not reach the general public until they had taken on the final form in which they were more or less approved (or definitely disapproved) by reasonable and cultured minds. Now the public deals with them itself—and a sorry mess it makes of it. Without training, without learning, without specialized knowledge, it flounders among the psychological fads and fancies of a doubting, disillusioned age. Modern atheism has gone far beyond the more or less negative form of it to which a polite world had grown accustomed. Like everything else it has increased in violence, thrown off restraint. The modern atheist is not content with mere disbelief: he is determined to carry his disbelief into open war.

We are assailed by every type of error, and of sometimes even attractive heresy: Marxism, Materialism, Rationalism, Logical Positivism: the young can take their choice, and only wake in later years to know that they have been duped—or maybe, more sadly still, never wake to truth again. But the philosophy which is as yet only on its way to us, and which has perhaps the greatest allure of any at the moment, and in the present mood of Man, is Existentialism. Ultimately it is bound to reach this country, although it may not reach it in quite the form which it takes abroad. The Holy Father does not warn unnecessarily, and it is not quite so simple in its essence as the ultra-modern and passing fashion which so many dismiss with a shrug of the shoulders.

Whether the philosophy of Nietzche in any way

influenced it is an open question. It is generally agreed that it began with the writings of Kierkegaard more than a hundred years ago, followed by those of Heidegger, born towards the end of the last century. Since the war of 1914, its progress in many European countries has been extraordinarily rapid. It thrives best in an atmosphere of disaster, of hopelessness; and should such moments ever come to us as a nation, this new and insidious doctrine of existence will surely follow closely behind.

Heidegger, the German, suddenly realized, in the trenches which were the scene of the first German defeat, what appeared to him to be the utter absurdity of life and death. It was the atmosphere of 1940-50 France which brought into the limelight the best known of the French Existentialists. Let us pray God that no such background will ever herald an English version of this doctrine of despair.

Pascal has said that there are in reality only two sorts of reasonable people: those who serve God with all their hearts because they know Him, and those who seek Him with all their hearts because they do not. For those of us who serve God there are always two ways of doing it, but one or the other we must choose. The fight has a double issue, but it is only one issue in the end. We can wrestle with men direct, out in the world, or we can wrestle with God for men, in secret and behind closed doors. Both are total war.

CHAPTER II

WEAPONS OF DEFENCE

EVEN should one want to belong to the company of
Pascal's reasonable people who serve God with all
their hearts because they know Him, or should one
go still further and choose the second way of serving Him,
which is in secret and in solitude, there is always an
earthly setting to the spiritual desire. This earthly setting, as regards contemplative nuns at all events, has
once again, in this latter half of the twentieth century,
become the preoccupation of the Holy See.

Now in all matters of perplexity in our convent, we
have instant recourse to Sister Imelda. She is our oldest
inhabitant, and a sure refuge in time of trouble. It
does not matter what the trouble may be, from sickness
to a new washer on a tap, she is able to advise. True,
the advice is sometimes a little reminiscent of the days
of balloons and high bicycles, and even sometimes, still
more impressively, of the days of the prophets, but it is
none the worse for that. Ours is, after all, not a modern
congregation, and we manage very well on the wisdom
of King Solomon.

During one memorable early spring, for instance,
when, instead of having influenza tactfully *en série* like
most of our friends in the world, our community suddenly and gallantly took the fence all together, Sister
Imelda was simply invaluable, not to say miraculous.

There were only two or three of us left on our feet, with
one postulant whom we suspected had secretly hoped

that she might succumb to it also, until unfortunately her temperature dropped abruptly to normal again, somewhat to her distress.

"Sister Imelda prayed for me," she sighed, as she resigned herself to becoming a nurse instead of a patient.

Other cures were equally remarkable. One of the novices announced that she felt sick, a sure beginning.

"Salt and water," decreed Sister Imelda cheerfully, "best to get it over." Instead, however, the illness was cured by the sister's having immediate recourse to the holy virtue of obedience. She providentially remembered that she had no permission to drink between meals. Whereupon the sickness left her. Indeed such marvels began to multiply as the days went on. It began to be enough to see Sister Imelda coming, to feel the beneficent effects of her presence. Another novice, not being quite sure how she felt, but quite sure that it was not as she should feel, prepared herself for a day or so in bed.

"I will take your temperature first," announced our kindly sister, producing the thermometer gingerly, for they have an unfortunate way of breaking on her which is most disconcerting.

"May I read it myself?" asked the novice hastily, for the most astounding figures have been known to come out of that instrument under the earnest gaze of Sister Imelda.

"Such a thing is never allowed, I am afraid, but I will use two pairs of spectacles."

"But then it will be at least 108," cried the novice aghast, and also recovered almost instantaneously, and without fuss, as is the way in the case of the best miracles.

Under these circumstances it is not to be wondered at that, when faced with a positive epidemic of new books of advice upon the general monastic situation of the post-war period, and particularly upon the apostolic constitution *Sponsa Christi* of Pope Pius XII, I should have had immediate recourse to the wisdom and experience of Sister Imelda.

The Constitution was first published in Rome on December 1st, 1950, and is considered by many to be the most important and far-reaching pronouncement upon the subject of the life of enclosed nuns (i.e. the *Moniales* of the Church) since the Council of Trent. On the 3rd September, 1563, during the final two-day session of that Council, a decree, in twenty-two chapters, on the reform of monks and nuns was approved and promulgated. *Sponsa Christi* is once more concerned, after a lapse of nearly four hundred years, with what is described as the renovation or renewal of the state of the cloistered nun.

It would be tedious for any but nuns themselves to go into all the details of the proposed methods of achieving this renewal, but what unquestionably emerges from the whole is that their mission is, in the eyes of the Church, not only still alive, but immensely and vividly alive, and that what is proposed is a wonderful enlargement of the conception of the contemplative vocation.

In the explanation of the document which was given at the end of the Congress of the Sacred Congregation of Religious on the day of its publication, Father Larraona used this phrase: "This renovation all good religious have at heart, desiring as they do to see their lives organized as efficiently as possible to meet the needs of the world of to-day. This is a work which our Holy Mother the Church herself intends to direct, and to carry out diligently and carefully."

The suggestion that enclosed contemplatives can do anything at all to meet the needs of to-day, and still more do it efficiently, will probably come as a profound shock to many. But let them take courage. It is the Church herself who proposes to see to the efficiency. What the world does not perhaps realize is that the actual religious are as aware of the situation as their critics can possibly be, and that it is a little superfluous to run up to a man busily engaged with buckets of water, and warn him excitedly that his chimney is on fire. Neither, on the other hand, is it necessary for him to get rid of all the fires in his house for ever after, and take solely to rugs and hot-water bottles in order to keep himself warm. The matter is quite simple in reality: all that he has to do is to sweep his chimney.

That is precisely what this Constitution proposes. The essentials of the enclosed religious life, as it is lived to-day, are maintained exactly as before; the only changes really suggested concern work—firstly, spiritual work, the apostolate of prayer and intercession, and secondly, economic work for the nuns' livelihood.

The formal characteristics of these *Moniales* are roughly, it is interesting to note, according to Canon Law four in number. Dedication to contemplative life: the taking of solemn vows: the observance of papal enclosure: and the obligation of the recitation of the divine office both in choir and individually. These can in no way be changed. But the non-essential details of the life, which have accumulated with the centuries, can very profitably be varied to meet the demands of modern existence in economic matters. Those demands had already perhaps led to some individual variations which were not too orthodox, and so the Church, taking pity on the well-meant efforts of the religious to move with the times, came to the rescue, as ever, with the perfect solution.

All the spiritual and contemplative essence of the life

she jealously guards and protects, but those purely material details of the framework of it, with which it is so difficult for enclosed communities to grapple effectively, she has settled *en bloc* so as to ensure a reasonable degree of uniformity while leaving every freedom for the particular requirements of each different Order. The most interesting of these concerns the apostolic work of *Moniales*. The actual words used are: "Nuns must realize that their vocation is wholly apostolic, unlimited by circumstances, by place, or time; it must extend everywhere and be exercised always in regard to all that in any way reflects on the honour of their Spouse, and which concerns the salvation of souls."

This is probably the sort of thing which enclosed nuns had been saying for some time in meek whispers, and which the little saint of Lisieux finally said quite loudly and unashamedly. But whereas the world has long since accepted her view of her own vocation, when it came to the ordinary enclosed nun, it was not perhaps quite so sure. However the words of the Church herself are unmistakable: "*Universalis apostolica vocatio*." Three principal means are suggested for the carrying out of the apostolate. The example of Christian perfection given to the world by the mere fact of the enclosed religious life; prayer; immolation.

The example of Christian perfection given to the world is perhaps intended to be on the lines of the silent testimony of Charles de Foucauld's desert communities, thus returning to the old tradition. The church spire against the evening sky while the Angelus rings out across the rippled sand. The prayer has its double form: the solemn choral recitation of the divine office "in the name of the Church" seven times a day, and the private prayer of intercession continuously offered. Behind that prayer, enriching it and seeking to add a note of urgency, of loving entreaty, to its humble appeal, lies the sacrifice of the enclosed religious life.

And that, in essence, is the whole story. For some Orders, the apostolic work may even include education, the nursing of the sick, and other activities of a similar nature, provided the enclosure of the nuns be effectually safeguarded according to the very precise regulations laid down.

Armed with all this information, a mass of good intentions, and two heavy tomes recently published in order to assist the feminine mind to carry them out, I went to find Sister Imelda in her workshop down at the bottom of the garden.

"Sister," I said firmly, taking a seat upon an upturned packing-case, "the moment has come for judicious advance. The Church says that we have got to be more up to date."

Sister Imelda stared. "Up to date?" she echoed. "What about? There is no date to God." Her voice was faintly shocked.

"No, but there is to the world. Postulants, it seems, come out of the world, and we have got to meet them half-way."

Sister Imelda glanced at the books under my arm. "If I were you," she said soothingly, "I would not read too much about it. It will only upset you."

"It *has* upset me," I replied grimly. "I understand a soul, and I understand a heart and feelings, but when it comes to all this psycho-business I just want to put my nose in the air and howl like a dog."

"Well, do," said Sister Imelda obligingly, and even, I thought, with a hopeful interest, "there's nobody here but me." Then as I did not respond: "I have never *really* understood what the psyche *is*?"

I drew one of the books from under my arm and

opened it at the chapter which I had been reading when
I decided that what *I* needed was a little fresh air and
Sister Imelda. "Here you are," I said, "just as it stands:
'The psyche is simply the product of brain-functioning
throughout our whole ancestral line, a precipitate of the
adaption-efforts and experiences of the phylogenetic suc-
cession'." Sister Imelda made a movement for all the
world as if she were pulling the communication-cord of a
train, and a sound like "Hi!" came out of her mouth, but
I did not stop; instead I opened the other book swiftly.
"'Human nature is composite. *Anima rationalis et caro
unus est homo.* The mind of man contains power not
only of a higher rational or spiritual grade, but also that
of a lower sensitive or organic order. The *psyche* is a
convenient term to denote this lower sensitive emotional part of the mind.'"

"When I was young and in the world," said Sister
Imelda, clutching at any conversational straw, "we never
talked about anything lower than the chest."

"'Knowledge of the rational and spiritual side of the
mind is supremely important for religious superiors.
Enough has been said already to show that some knowledge of the devious ways of the lower sensitive organic
psyche is important also if the bewildering varieties of
human behaviour are to be understood and loved.'"

"Neither," said Sister Imelda with sudden decision.
"If you are going to understand and love that sort of
stuff, and to teach it to your novices, I don't know what
you will make of them, but I can tell you that it will not
be Carmelites."

"You mistake," I said blandly, "it is not me teaching
this sort of stuff, it is this sort of stuff teaching me."

"Don't let it," admonished Sister Imelda sternly,
"Don't let it. Psyche!—Pish! Anyway I thought she
was a goddess."

"You remind me of the story of a woman who was globe-trotting. She remarked one day that she had seen a most beautiful statue of Psish in one of the art-galleries. After a moment or two of pained reflection, her acquaintance suggested that she might possibly be referring to Psyche? 'Oh,' she replied airily, 'some say Psyche and some say Psish. I say Psish'."

Sister Imelda however was looking troubled. "Is *Sponsa Christi* really like that?"

"*Sponsa Christi?*" I questioned. "Of course it is not. *Sponsa Christi* came straight from the Holy Father and is one of the loveliest things that has ever been written from our point of view."

"Then you keep to that," advised Sister Imelda with relief, picking up her pot of paste, "and let the psychologists explain all the rest to each other. Don't you worry about modern postulants. Leave them alone and they'll come home, bringing their tails behind them." I got up to go and I admit that I felt better. "Leave the books with me," she coaxed, "I should find them so very useful." She eyed them with undoubted satisfaction which, considering all the things she had just said about them, appeared rather strange.

"I thought you did not like them much!"

"They are beautiful books," said Sister Imelda, doing a sudden *volte face* and holding out her two hands for them, "thick, and large, and fat, and heavy." I admit that they are, but she had not seemed to regard them quite in that light a few minutes earlier. I looked at her suspiciously; there is usually method in Sister Imelda's madness.

"But you told me not to read too much of them—what is the difference between us?" The hermit smiled sweetly.

"The difference," she said, "lies in the application."

She weighed first one, then the other, in her hands with the utmost satisfaction. "*Deo gratias*," she said, which is our way of assuming holy and religious proprietorship over something which does not belong to us, particularly if the other person, to whom it does belong, does not altogether wish to part with it. "They are *just* what I was needing."

"But you said. . . ."

"I am sticking the pictures on to our next-year's Christmas cards," she whispered confidentially, "I have hundreds to do and they need pressing. There is nothing fat enough in the library to hold them, but these are just right, I can do the whole of them at one press." She beamed at me, hugging the volumes resolutely. I thought of the learned and pious authors, and of what their feelings would be if they could see her, and I am sorry to say that I laughed. At that she knew that she had won the day in more ways than one.

"You can't alter this life really, you know, not enough to make any difference. You can call things by different names, and you can shift the weight a little this way or that to suit each generation, but contemplatives are contemplatives all the world over, and in every century. You can talk to them about their psyches if you think it will help them, but in the end you will only have told them the same things that we were told about our souls. Those who want God, will stay for love of God, and those who do not, will go home again, but it has always been like that."

"But it is true that vocations are getting fewer, Sister."

"Those who love God to that point may be fewer, but nothing we do can alter that either," she said. She looked at me with her kind, shrewd, yet innocent eyes. "Teach them to love God and they will stay all right. You can't expect the love of God not to have slipped a little during

the war and after—even long after. That is all that is
the matter. Love of the neighbour, oh yes, that is still
there. Missionaries, and nurses, and the adventures of
factory-apostles. Those are the fashion nowadays and a
very good fashion it is. Just what the world needs. But
changing our life would not alter that fashion in the
least after all; for the moment it is set in that direction.
It will swing back again, and perhaps sooner than the
world expects."

" And meanwhile? "

" Meanwhile we wait and trust God. The vocations
may not be many, but they are there, and the fewness
of them may in the end be the very thing which becomes
the attraction. People get tired after a while of doing
just what everybody else is doing. It is exciting to be
a pioneer—but the more pioneers the less exciting."

I looked at the volumes again. "I really think I ought
to read them right through," I said, " they are composed
especially to teach us how to deal with modern difficulties. . . ."

" Well, you come down and deal with your difficulties
here then," advised Sister Imelda cheerfully. " You will
feel better about them than indoors; it is wonderful what
a difference a run round the garden makes to the psyche,
particularly the lower part of it; and meanwhile I will
take great care of the books for you."

As I stepped out of the courtyard into the garden, I
looked back. She was turning the pages of the fattest
with absorbed attention while between each leaf she
carefully dropped a freshly-mounted Christmas picture.
All is grist that comes to the mill of Sister Imelda, and
even psychology has its uses.

CHAPTER III

OURSELVES AS WE ARE

ROGER Troisfontaines makes a most interesting classification of men in general. Psychologically he divides them into three categories.[1] Firstly, leaders and organizers. Secondly, poets, dreamers, and introspectives generally who, without taking the initiative in the actual direction of events, are nevertheless keenly alive to their repercussions, to their various underlying qualities, and meditate profoundly upon their lessons. Thirdly, a class including diplomats and scholars who, with lucid, imperturbable brains draw, from the most moving incidents, only an abstract theory.

These three can alternatively be divided into the emotional-active people who make history; the emotional-inactive people who merely feel it; and the cold-actives who think it. So, according to his classification, we are all by nature either engaged in acting, or re-acting, or deducing, unless we belong to the completely apathetic type which closes its eyes altogether to life and its implications. Thus we each of us, except those belonging to the last-named category, draw from our own personal experience and reactions a sort of rough philosophy of life, and that philosophy will take its colour from our natural character.

Between these broad distinctions, however, there lie all the shades of infinitely varying degrees comprised within the three categories. He explains that, taking it

[1] *Existentialisme et Pensée Chrétienne.* R. Troisfontaines. p. 10.

as a whole, it can be said that the second type cannot escape from subjectivity any more than the cold-actives can from objectivity. It will be with difficulty that the former will regard the world except in relation to the individual, or that the latter will bring themselves to allow, in their frigid calculations, for the intrusion of the human element.

It is as well to take account of ourselves as we are, and so far as the ideological war of this century is concerned, the first and the second of these classes are those which mainly concern us. Theories are very well in their own department, but the theorists themselves are apt to get in the way when bombs, spiritual or otherwise, are falling. If we are to take account of ourselves and our characteristics as we are to-day, we must admit that the events of the present century have not made greatly for stability. With the whole world rocking around one, it is not easy to keep both one's head and one's feet.

An admiral was once explaining that if one wished to avoid sea-sickness when at sea (which we all of us did), the great thing was to avoid being paralysed by the cold. "Look after the extremities," he muttered several times, wagging his head, "look after the extremities and the rest of you will be all right." We are most of us engaged in trying to look after our extremities nowadays, it seems to me, but not with marked success.

Modern education, so spasmodic, so interrupted for one cause or another over which the unfortunate student has no control, is also no doubt partly to blame. The late Professor Whitehead gives a perfect definition of stability and mental grasp when he speaks of the "priceless habit of looking for an exact point and of sticking to it when found". "The Middle Ages," he remarks, "formed one long training of the intellect of Western Europe in the sense of order. There may have been some deficiency in respect to practice. But the idea never for a moment lost its grip. . . . It needs but a sentence to point out how the habit of definite, exact thought was implanted in the European mind by the long dominance of scholastic logic and scholastic divinity."[2]

From across the Atlantic comes the same warning. "The mediæval University," writes Dr. Hutchins, "had a principle of unity. It was theology . . . without theology or metaphysics an university cannot exist. Both are missing to-day. And with them has gone any intelligible basis of the study of man in his relations to other men. The truths of ethics, for example, are now merely common-sense teachings about how to get along in the world."[3]

This is a genuine warning, for if we once allow our will and our sense of duty to be affected by expediency, or merely by our reactions to other people's conduct, we are on a slippery slope as regards stability of purpose. It does not perhaps sound very important, yet if, for example, we allow ourselves to be noticeably influenced by rudeness, we may also find ourselves dangerously open to the influence of an often foolish flattery.

If the individuals of a nation are, as a whole, taking their stand upon the firm ground of right and wrong, the general policy of that nation will do the same; this has its world effect. The danger is that, if the individuals begin to slacken in their beliefs, the policy may continue for some little time on its own momentum, while the thing which was its real foundation and driving-force has melted away unawares and no longer exists.

This is the spiritual and psychological disaster which modern Christians have to try at all costs to avert. For no country will for long continue to strain, and endea-

[2] *Science and the Modern World.* Professor Whitehead.
[3] *The Higher Learning in America.* R. M. Hutchins (Univ. Chicago).

C

vour, and sacrifice, for something in which its individual
citizens do not believe. For a time, and superficially, it
may continue to live on the catchwords of the past, but
when the real crisis comes, the empty slogans will no
longer hold its disillusioned people. We must beware
of living, as Renan phrased it many years ago, on the
perfume of an empty vase.

Things which used to be regarded as firm decisions in
life are now so often merely regarded as experiments.
Careers, vocations, marriage: all have taken on a temporary aspect in the eyes of the younger generation. The
change, of course, is in where we place our decision,
not in the decision itself. We still make our decisions
with a good deal of vigour, only not at the right moment.
The decision used to precede the project, which was
then carried out; now it follows on the heels of the experi-
ment, and usually brings it to an end.

For some women, at least, life seems to be viewed as a
perpetual bargain-hunt. Its possibilities have the same
irresistible attraction for them as a sale catalogue. Even
if they have no particular use for a thing, still if they
think that it is going cheap—above all if they think that
somebody else wants it—they must set out in feverish
pursuit. From this arises a whole series of cross-pur-
poses. The first is a cross-purpose with themselves,
marked by a growing vagueness as to what they really
want in life. The second is a cross-purpose with everybody else, since people naturally suppose that they want
what they have obviously set out to get. And the third,
and infinitely the most important, is a cross-purpose with
God, whose eternal purposes they have completely rele-
gated to the background in their own hunt for new and
eccentric fashions at the sale-counter of life.

Whatever else we may bargain about, or for, or with,
at least we need not trade with our ideals. No cheap

ideal was ever worth the money we paid for it, nor the time we spent on it, no matter how little either may have been. For our purse has a bottom, and our time an end, and when we have spent all of both that was ours, we shall be sad indeed if we find that, unawares, we have frittered away the one priceless possession which we might have had for nothing, and that is God's love.

Contrary as it may be to the present practice and to present ways of thinking, let us stick to our purposes and to our early conceptions. For the people who can keep clear and untarnished the visions of their youth usually make a quiet, coherent success of life. They may not necessarily be very brilliant, but they go on consistently following a kind of sub-conscious spiritual and mental plan; they develop along certain lines which seemed to them in youth to lead towards the end they wanted to reach; and maturity finds them still walking steadily in the same direction. This is, of course, almost the precise opposite of the modern admiration for inconstancy, its delight in improvisation, in the cult of the mood of the moment, and the unending pursuit of the fashions of next year.

It is immensely right to change in the minor things of life; to see the world; to try one's hand at this and that; to be open to the influence of everything that is beautiful and invigorating; to move with the times. One era melts into the next. It is certainly unpleasant to be living in between two, as we are; still, let us go on hopefully into what follows. It will not last any more than this, and there is always heaven at the end. But in the choice of basic principles and deeper loves we shall do well to cultivate a sense of steadfastness and solidity. The more firmly we are established both spiritually and psychologically, the more gay and light-hearted can we afford to be over the unending trifles which go to make up our existence. The gift of balance, of sense of proportion, is perhaps a greater gift than we appreciate, and is reflected back on other people also in the unselfish outlook of its possessor.

The unselfish person is never either a square or a round peg in any hole. The square has corners, and the round deficiencies, unknown to unselfish people. With amazement we shall watch them puff themselves out and tuck themselves in most obligingly to fit exactly any hole in which they happen to find themselves. We are fortunate indeed if that chances to be the hole next to ours.

We shall discover, among other things, that they are not given to choosing—either with God or with other people. We all know that most anguished type of spiritual person who spends her prayer-time in imagining God as offering her perpetually recurring contrasts. Joy —suffering: health—sickness: prosperity—misfortune: good fame—humiliation. She goes through tortures in the endeavour to brace herself to choose the worse in each case. But why choose at all? Why not leave it to God, and take cheerfully whatever He sends? When suffering comes, let us try to be generous; when happiness is our portion, do not let us forget the gratitude. Let us try to be patient and gentle under humiliation, and to laugh at the praise which is so inappropriate to us. Let us, in short, say quite simply to God: " Not my choice—Yours. Always, first and last, what You want. My only choice is Yours."

In the matter of the spiritual war in which we are engaged, we shall find that our religion must be a philosophy, as well as a faith, if it is to hold its own among modern conditions and with its modern antagonists. Our Faith is sufficient for us, we know, but we cannot expect others to be convinced by something of which they know nothing and which they have not as yet received. It is for us to show them just why they have to become Christians. The appeal of all these new theories of life offered to the present generation is that they contain *ideas*: they offer to fill a void in us. Half the time, people do not trouble to get as far as the practical consequences of the ideals at all; it is the thought alone which catches and holds the fancy. But that is not enough if we are fighting for God. We must go deeper.

Taken as a whole Man does not change greatly in three fundamental relationships, that is (1) in his relation to God (2) to others (3) to himself. Faith in God, if we have it at all, does not alter its essentials with the passing of the centuries. Love never changes its essence, although the modes of its expression may vary. In spite of all the psychiatrists in the world, we remain to ourselves what primitive man was to himself—an enigma; but an enigma which we are constantly trying to solve, as he did also, and to express to our own and other minds in intelligible terms. Hence philosophies: hence the philosophers who make them. Their charm for us is that they hold up the mirror of their individual thought and personality, and sometimes, with unexpected delight, for a moment we meet not their, but our own, reflection. Now it is one vogue, now another, a shifting kaleidoscope of hope and questing. But through it all there is to be distinguished the firm, undeviating message of Christian teaching, founded on divine truth.

The danger of allowing our fancy to be caught by attractive theories and adopting them, without following them out to their practical consequences, is obvious. Our young people—even sometimes Catholic young people— play with the ideas of Marxism, Logical Positivism and Existentialism, while they would be horrified to live as Marxists or Existentialists live. That is why Douglas Hyde, and those who have been what may be termed practising Communists, warn us that Communism must not be regarded as a philosophy, but as a religion. The same is true of the other two. The fact is that all religions are philosophies, while most philosophies tend to turn into religions—or irreligions. In the old days Faith alone was enough, and so it is still when it is only ourselves in question; but for the sake of others we must also clearly understand the basis of our Faith. If to a philosophy one must oppose a contrary philosophy, then to an irreligion one must oppose, even more, a positive and arguable religion.

One of the main points made by Existentialist writers is that there can be no direct knowledge for us of the soul of another. We can only come to know his mind by a process of analogy. We believe that his body is inhabited by a spirit similar to ours, merely because we see that his appearance and behaviour are similar to ours. But we can have no certainty on the point. This is obviously an absurdity, but it does draw attention to something else which may be more true. We can never be sure of the *exact value* to another of the words which we use, nor of how far they will convey to him precisely what is in our own mind. For we all have a trick of taking other people's experiences, and translating them at our own level. That may be either above or below theirs, but in either case what they have said or experienced will not mean quite to us what it did to them.

Herein can be seen the importance of *living* our Faith. Our words may be misunderstood, but the happiness which surrounds us, the peace which our belief reflects back on to our surroundings, the courage given by our trust in God, these can never be misunderstood. Sooner or later they will convince. At least they will convince of this much: that we have something which other people have not; something which keeps us steady, keeps us happy, under adverse circumstances. Sooner or later, those whom we meet will try to find out what that something is. Sooner or later, if we pray enough for them, they will succeed.

CHAPTER IV

THE IDEA SHOP

THE gossamer threads of a late autumn frost spangled the bushes on either side of the path as I walked towards the courtyard and Sister Imelda's workshop. I wanted her advice about a leaking tap, but it was not about taps that we talked when finally I arrived at her open door. She was all mixed up for the moment with fowls and Anthony the Cat. Straw littered the floor in every direction, and the chickens scratched and shrieked simultaneously, while Anthony dashed in and out between their legs in an exceedingly upsetting fashion. Sister Imelda, I could see, was a little upset too. Fowls' nerves are not of the strongest, and those of ours had evidently completely given way. Meanwhile Anthony was enjoying himself very much; for once he had allowed himself to unbend.

"Chick, chick, chick, come!" called Sister Imelda above the wild cackling. "Anthony—stop, stop!" Unfortunately the chickens stopped and Anthony came; he came with a flying leap which sent every bird into the air and himself straight into my chest.

"You are a bad cat," I remarked, clasping him however firmly to my heart. Anthony immediately became as soft as velvet and as innocent as a kitten just learning to lap. His eyes were round and melting, like wet blackberries in the sun. Anthony has several pairs of eyes which he uses according to his mood. There are his green, professional, there's-a-mouse-in-the-wainscot eyes which precede the flurry of a chase of some sort; and his golden-glory eyes which he keeps for Sunday afternoons, and for all those other more ceremonial occasions when he wishes to remind us that cats are very marvellous and sacred animals and should be treated only with the deepest respect. And there are his soft, shiny black eyes which I like best, and which he only uses for thinking. Sometimes they are narrowed into long almond slits, and then one knows that he has retired altogether into another world where no human may follow, while he dreams of the civilizations of centuries past, in the days when his ancestors lived in the palaces of kings and ate from golden dishes. And sometimes, as now, they are merely the soft, kittenish eyes which I am afraid he saves up for thinking how best he can get his own way.

"I will hold him while you remove the chickens," I said to Sister Imelda, "I came for your advice." She swept them in front of her into the courtyard; Anthony quivered, then remembered that it was a moment for propitiation not hunting; with a few brisk movements of the broom she reduced the floor to order.

"I was unpacking a crate," she explained apologetically, "and I forgot the door was open. It is real wheatstraw—trust a fowl to find that out!"

I put Anthony down. Perceiving that the fun was over, he strolled after the chickens into the frosty morning air. Suddenly another sound caught my ear. "What's that noise?" I asked, listening.

"Sawing," said Sister Imelda nonchalantly.

"Sawing? Who? Firewood?"

"The postulant. Sawing carver's blocks for me."

"Oh!" I remarked blankly; then, as awful possibilities loomed up before me: "Does she like sawing?" I enquired anxiously.

"Didn't ask," said Sister Imelda, obviously not interested in the postulant's feelings. "Keeps her warm."

"Well, yes, it does. Still . . ."

"Nobody ever asked me whether I liked sawing," said Sister Imelda firmly, but I thought a little on the defensive, "and I am not going to ask anybody either. I don't mind mentioning their psyches occasionally, if you think it helps, but not their sensations." There was a thus-and-no further note in her voice which no one could mistake.

The sound ceased; footsteps approached; another moment and the postulant herself stood in the arch of the doorway. In her hand she carried some blocks of wood and her cheeks were bright pink.

"*Deo gratias*, Sister," I said, as she put the blocks down and then, as if impelled by some irresistible force: "Do you like sawing?"

"Oh, yes." I breathed again. "Keeps me warm," she added.

"So it does," I agreed brightly, and the three of us sank into silence. Sister Imelda broke it at last.

"But you *would* do it just the same if it made you cold, wouldn't you?" she enquired pathetically. The kind of 'adaptation' advised for what is called "*la religieuse d'aujourd'hui*" is a constant source of worry and bewilderment to her. There is no *aujourd'hui* about Sister Imelda's type of sanctification.

"Oh, yes," said the postulant and smiled.

Sister Imelda became visibly easier in mind—her psyche settled down. "You can always offer any little discomforts of that sort for the intentions of some priest," she explained casually, but watching the effect out of the corner of one eye.

"Perhaps," I put in, mindful of the book, now bulging with Sister Imelda's best Christmas cards, and not wishing to rush things with the young, "you have as yet no special priest for whom to pray?"

Sister Elizabeth smiled again. "Oh, yes, as a matter of fact I have," she announced quite triumphantly. "Not one I really know—but still. . . ."

"Is he a parish-priest?" asked Sister Imelda, putting down her little saw, and interested at last. She dearly loves a parish-priest and all his intentions.

"I don't know. I honestly don't. I only met him in a train going to Rome. He said he lived there, and he guessed somehow that I was going to enter religion, and he promised to say a Mass for me. Then he asked me to pray for him." Surprised at so many words in a row, she blushed and once more relapsed into silence.

"You can pray for him just as well without knowing who he is; we don't need to know the names of the people we pray for."

"Oh, no." Suddenly she became reminiscent. "They had funny ideas about things, those people," she remarked with a little laugh, "nuns, and careers, and all their new sorts of philosophy. The one thing I am afraid they had not got, practically any of them, was a religion. What can you *do* about people like that?" she ended helplessly. "*I* was no good at them."

"Do? Do about them?" Sister Imelda eyed her sternly. "What you *are* doing, of course. What do you *think* you are doing when you are sawing and all that? You don't imagine you are just cutting up blocks of wood, and washing altar-linen, and getting frozen fingers for fun, do you?"

"Oh, no," said the postulant hastily.

"Well, then! . . . As to the funny ideas themselves, that is nothing new. It always happens after times of great material restriction." Sister Imelda spoke as if she had lived in three centuries at least at different periods of the world's history; we listened respectfully. Sister Elizabeth leaned against the doorpost, I noticed, but by mutual consent we let her lean. Ordinarily Carmelites do not lean much upon anything except God. But she would learn with time. Sister Imelda proceeded, eyes turned resolutely away from the door.

"When people cannot get what they want from ordinary shops, and all their things begin to wear out and there are no new ones to replace them, and everything gets dustier and dingier as the months go by, and there seems no hope of anything new or plentiful ever again: in the end they get sick of it, you see, and off they go to the idea-shop."

"The what?" we exclaimed simultaneously.

"The idea-shop," repeated Sister Imelda placidly, "where you get the new ideas from, you know, which console you for all the other new things which you want and can't get."

"What sort of ideas?" I asked at last.

"It depends upon who you are and what you like, and where the particular shortage hits you. If you love freedom, for instance, and travelling, and getting about, and the restrictions cramp your physical movements, then you turn Communist, Existentialist, or any other sort of *ist* which happens to be handy, and which you think lets you loose mentally. If you are a religious sort of person, you may become a Buddhist or a Theosophist, or one of those sort of *ists*, it doesn't matter which, and you soar through space in imagination until you come to Nirvana, or somewhere like that, where it is of no importance what you can get or not get, because you have no more desires anyway. Communists are to have no desires either, I understand, when they reach their synthesis, which will not be in our time, because then they will only have to stretch out a hand and there will be all the earth's wealth within its grasp. So convenient. But if you are a Christian, of course," her voice changed, "you just stay where you are, and pray that the shortages will soon be over, and remember that Our Lord went short of everything when He was on earth for our sake."

Sister Elizabeth and I stared at each other; she had, I noticed, resumed a completely vertical position.

"Where did you get all that from?" I ventured at last.

"My psyche, of course," said Sister Imelda complacently, and at that the postulant gave it up. She rocked helplessly. I glanced towards the spot where the books from Rome and Paris reposed, and wondered whether we were applying the principles quite rightly. Did postulants rock suitably nowadays at the utterances of their mistresses? In our day we did not. But before I could put my doubt into words, Sister Elizabeth spoke.

"I must say I like your girl-friend," she announced, looking at me, "we speak the same language."

If you do not draw the line somewhere, then where are you to draw the line? I was quite sure that that at least was not in the book.

"Sister Elizabeth," I said severely, then added a hasty 'dear' in case I sounded too harsh, which the manual most particularly recommends us to avoid, "you really cannot refer to the assistant novice-mistress as my girl-friend."

"Oh, I *am* sorry."

"She has been fifty years in religion: long before you were even born."

"You wouldn't think it," said Sister Elizabeth tactfully, "twenty-five at the very most."

The corners of Sister Imelda's mouth quivered and I

was afraid that she was going to smile in the wrong
place.

"Saint Gertrude had it revealed to her that she
received a special grace of some kind, I forget which,
for drawing back and bowing respectfully when she met
an old religious."

"She does," said Sister Imelda, suddenly and incon-
veniently taking the postulant's part just when I was
getting on so nicely, "she is really most respectful. You
see, Sister," she turned towards the doorway, "what she
means is that there is a sort of atmosphere about religious
life which is really rather essential to it. It is so essential, in fact, that you can almost say it is part of it,
just as pale grey mist is part of an autumn morning, and
October must have russet beech leaves somewhere in it
if it is to feel like October. If we were standing here in
sweltering sunshine, we should not know that we were
nearly into the winter, and if we were to use all the expressions and language of the world, we should not know
that we were in religion. If we forget that we are in
religion, out here in the garden, Sister, very soon we
shall forget that we are in religion even in the choir. I
do not mean in the least that we should forget God or
religion itself, any more than people in the world do,
but we should forget that we are *in* it: part of it, belonging to it, never for a moment coming out of it. Have I
made sense of what I mean at all?"

"Oh, yes."

There was a moment's silence. Books, I decided,
were no good at all when it came to real people. They
were full of their own theories, and very good theories
too, but they never took into account what the other
people were going to say or think. Still . . . The
sound of the bell drifted over from the convent building.
Sister Elizabeth's eyes grew dreamy. They had that

almost other-worldly look which sometimes comes into them.

"Methinks," she said, speaking slowly and painstakingly, "that yonder bell ringeth us to meate—I mean fishe—and that we must een goe and answer its calle."

We got up. Speechlessly I waved her towards the path; Sister Imelda followed behind looking pleased but mystified. In single file we walked between the beds of chrysanthemums and red berberis, still lightly touched with frost. I felt a little pull at my arm. "Was it Chaucer?" whispered Sister Imelda in an awed· voice.

"No—Elizabethan."

The back of the postulant assumed an even more propitiatory curve. I had meant her to hear and she had; nevertheless I decided to consult the book again, alone and in secret, after dinner. I would be careful not to displace any of the cards lest they should betray me, although after all it was my book if it were anyone's, and I had a perfect right to look at it as often as I liked.

We reached the choir and the cantor began the *De Profundis* which takes us in procession to the refectory. I felt that the *De Profundis* was a singularly appropriate and understanding psalm. We finished grace and took our seats. The postulant, I thought, still looked a little other-worldish, as well she might.

That night, however, I sat down and wrote to a priest in Rome whom I had known for many years, long before I entered religion. Rome, I reflected, was the place where the books came from. Perhaps they knew more about them there than I did. At all events I could but try.

"I understand there are certain 'adaptations' of the religious life which are being advocated in order to meet the needs" (Temperaments? Mentalities? Psyches? —Psyche, that was the word of course!) "to meet the psyches of modern postulants. I have bought some of the volumes, but I must admit that they have not left me much clearer on our own novitiate. The theories are marvellously well thought out, but I cannot but feel that those who dealt with them had not met our latest postulant. They had met other postulants, of course, perhaps Italian or French or Dutch, but not ours. She is an excellent aspirant but, religiously considered, she never reacts according to their assumptions. Dealing with her is like talking French out of a conversation manual. Someone says 'Have you the dictionary of my uncle?' and the other person replies, 'No, but my aunt has a cold in the head.' It never says what they do after that, or how the conversation ends. By the way, Sister Elizabeth says that she prays every day for some priest who lives in Rome but she does not know his name. She met him in the summer, it seems, when she was there last, and he promised to say a Mass for her intention. Well, he gets his prayers all right, but do try and find out more for me about these new adaptations and how to apply them. It is the *application* which worries me. . . ."

CHAPTER V

ATHEISM THEN AND NOW

THE nineteenth century produced a good many foolish optimists in the matter of the future of man: a happy future, to be based entirely upon his own merits, irrespective of divine grace and the merits of Jesus Christ. Evolution was the great word, and if it did not succeed in covering a multitude of sins it certainly covered a great amount of nonsense. Such writers as Herbert Spencer, Herschel, and later H. G. Wells, professed to believe with an almost naïve faith in the ultimate perfection of man, following on an ordered and inevitable progress of the whole human race. Looking round the world as it is to-day, it certainly would call for a great deal of optimism to adopt any theory of that sort, too crude for the present day mind, but there are others, no less misleading, to take its place.

Most of these philosophers came to see a different vision as they neared the end of their lives, and it was a sad vision for them. Renan began to realize that the collapse of supernatural belief, to which he had looked forward so gaily in his earlier days, would be followed by the collapse of the whole moral code, and would possibly make but a depressing mess of his pictured Utopia. When Wells wrote his last message to the world to which he had preached for so many decades, it was a message of despair. " Mind at the end of its tether," was how he expressed it, without realizing that the mind chiefly at the end of its tether was his own. His theories left the Chris-

D

tian mind just where it had always been, which is, perennially, at no end at all but at the beginning of everything.

There was once a small girl who was faced by a large State School Inspector, bent on making her an early convert to Darwinism. When he had finished all that he had to say, she replied politely but firmly: "Well, you may be descended from a monkey, but God made me." As Professor Eddington cheerfully remarks: "Dismiss the idea that natural law can swallow up religion; it cannot even tackle the multiplication-table single-handed!"

Probably the most attractive of all the pagan writers of that period, and of the first half of this century, was Bernard Shaw. His paganism was of so attractive a type, in fact, that he did an almost incredible amount of harm with it—which may the Lord forgive him for the sake of his own perhaps not so unbelieving end, and the whimsical irresponsibility of that brilliant brain of his. Bernard Shaw, one sometimes felt, was unable to resist the mocking charm of his own fancies. Unfortunately a good many others were unable to resist it either, and it was appallingly dangerous. He did a devastating work by upsetting the faith of innumerable young people during the first thirty years of the twentieth century. By youth as a whole, he was taken *au grand sérieux*; read, re-read, quoted, followed; and he may well be responsible for much of the mild atheism which overtook that generation in England.

Unfortunately neither the worship of Shaw nor the unbelief which it engendered has yet come to an end. Shortly after his death some lines were published which unconsciously gave the picture, in the minds of his admirers, not only of G.B.S.[1] himself, but of the trend of his philosophy.[1]

[1] Edward Shanks.

Now silence!—yet to-night he sits
By Shakespeare's side, agog to try
That first-hand battle of their wits
Which makes it well worth while to die.

That is the degree of subtle insult to God which has been reached, and which most of us seem to accept almost as a matter of course and without turning a hair at it. It is worth while to die in order to see, not God, but Shakespeare, and to hear him arguing with Bernard Shaw. There is our heaven. It is so polite, so apparently intellectual, so tragically and insidiously casual, that half the people who come in contact with that sort of thing appear to be unaware of the direction in which it leads. The more violent and decided forms of irreligion, of which there are also many to-day, are much less dangerous in their way, since one can scarcely play with them unawares.

For the non-Catholic Christian, however, one must admit that this view of heaven (if it is to heaven that the verses refer) may not sound quite so strange as it does to Catholic ears. For among many good Christians there seems to be something of that attitude towards God in their view of eternity. "You will see father and mother again," is the kind of comfort and encouragement that is honestly judged fitting for the last moments on earth of some loved one, and offered in perfectly good faith and sincerity. This latter view is certainly pious in intention, while the one expressed in the verses has no sort of piety attached to it, but at the root of both lies the same blind and tragic ignorance of the real nature of God, and of our relationship to Him.

It is true that many a professed atheist is in reality not so much rejecting God, as a false idea of Him which he has conceived. L'Abbé Grevillot says,[2] in speaking of Péguy, for instance, that he grew up under the instruction of both his parish priest and his schoolmaster, without perceiving the contrary nature of their teaching; but, arrived at adolescence, he found himself obliged to choose between them, and he chose the atheism of his schoolmaster because it appeared to him as a doctrine of liberty and progress. He rejected the belief in God of his parish priest, only because it seemed to him no more than a servile fear of hell.

In reality he was balancing not God at all, but two human values, freedom and servility, and choosing the one which seemed to him the finer. It was not until much later in life that he came to realize that the values which he loved from the depths of his soul were completely entwined with faith in a God of hope. "Thus," says Père Grevillot, "at the very moment when he was calling himself an atheist, he was only rejecting a false idea of God and he was already *en route* for the true God."

Maritain emphasises the same point when he remarks that there are many pseudo-atheists who believe that they do not believe in God, but who in reality unconsciously believe in Him, because the God whom they deny is not God at all, but something else.[3]

There is, however, nothing of this in the atheism of the Existentialists. Theirs is a positive creed and the outcome of a bitter and undisguised hatred of God. The philosophy has, in fact, been described quite simply as "the world as seen by an atheist". It is this attitude which we are primarily fighting in our present-day war of the spirit.

There are, of course, two distinct trends in Existentia-

[2] *Les Grands Courants de la Pensée Contemporaine.* Grevillot. p. 59.
[3] *La Signification de l'Atheisme Contemporain.* Maritain. p. 9, etc.

lism: trends so widely separated that they can scarcely, one is tempted to think, be called logically by the same name; yet, because they *are* called by the same name, the second and milder form of this fashionable philosophy becomes also suspect. Taking, for one moment, the atheist form of it only, it rests, and must necessarily rest, upon a fundamental denial of the existence of God. For, to those who profess it, God would be an obstacle to the complete liberty of man which they claim, and the attainment of which seems to them the principal goal of life.

Their idea of liberty, following the Nietzschean tradition, is bound up with the theory that Man, in order to be sovereignly free and independent, must, so to speak, become his own God. He has to create for himself his own being, his own ideas, his own values. In order to do this effectually, he is obliged first to destroy all that he has *received* and, as it were, to create a new self from the negation of the old. In the Existentialist sense it is clear that, in order to build, one must destroy all in one-self which already exists, because *to build upon* what one had been already accorded, would be, in effect, to admit the existence of God. This is, indeed, a passing, as Père Grevillot remarks, from atheism *à la Française,* which seeks to safeguard the old traditional moral code, to the much more radical atheism of the German philosophers of the last century.

According to Maritain, atheism can be divided into two classes at the present time, negative and positive.[4] Negative atheism rejects the idea of God, but that idea is only replaced by a void or emptiness. It is a simple absence. Incidentally, of course, that absence does confer upon man a sort of liberty, but as an effect rather than as an object. Positive atheism, on the contrary, is

[4] *La significance de l'Atheisme Contemporain.* Maritain. p. 10, etc.

an active fight against God and all that reminds man of God, and at the same time a despairing effort to reconstruct the whole human world of thought and values in accordance with such a state of declared war against the Deity.   Such positive atheism is to be found in the philosophy of Nietzche, Heidegger, the French atheist exponents of Existentialism, or again in the revolutionary atheism of Marx and of Dialetic Materialism.

Maritain classes contemporary atheism, of the more intellectual sort, as a positive and absolute atheism, and he regards it as unprecedented in history because it is, for the first time, accompanied by a violent demand that it shall be definitely *lived* by its disciples, with intent to change the face of the earth.   This is the measure of the danger which we are facing.   It is no mere intellectual conviction, it is a thing of the spirit and the heart and the will.   The birth of this attitude in any soul can be no casual, passing event.   It does not spring from carelessness but from a fierce and deliberate resolution.   The positive atheist has continually to fight in himself any traces of belief in the transcendent which threatens to surge up again in his mind from time to time, just as the Christian may have to fight at certain moments doubts which threaten his peace of soul.

Just as the latter fight establishes and strengthens faith, so the former destroys inexorably all supernatural belief. The fight is a conscious fight.   It is not merely a forgetting of God, it is a fixed and deliberate denial of God. The soul is making an act of faith in reverse—faith in a world and a system eternally devoid of God and of the supernatural.   It is a complete refusal to accept things as they were created, and a determination to create, instead, a world of one's own.

Now, in the spiritual war in which we are engaged, the

saint does precisely the same thing. People are very busy nowadays trying to establish a likeness, to prove a common starting-point, for saints and all sorts of other people: criminals, for instance, and lunatics, and degenerates. This, we are told, renders the saints more accessible, although I have never been able quite to see why, the rest of us not being exclusively criminals and lunatics. Still, it is true that in this particular case the saint does do the same thing although not for the same reason. He too breaks with the world as it is, in order to live a new life in Christ. His, also, is in a sense war against the whole fabric of society. But it is a war undertaken in order to bring nearer the day when there shall indeed be a new heaven and a new earth; the day of the unopposed reign of Christ.

It is in this battle for God that we ordinary Christians have also to take our part by resolutely opposing our philosophy to that of the pagans. We say resolutely because it is just that lack of definite outline in contemporary life which is so bewildering to the young. The cause of it is not easy to find: the remedy even less so. Nearly all these modern philosophies treat truth as purely relative. They substitute for the old conception of principles and values which were superior to time, and had their foundations firmly laid in the transcendent, the idea of truth conditioned by the changing forms of history and evolution. Everything, they argue, is in a state of flux; therefore that which is quite true and moral for me to-day is based only on a shifting standard; to-morrow that truth and that moral code may be changed and modified by the passing of events.

Is it strange that, built upon such unstable premises, modern characters tend to be a little unstable themselves? But Christianity still rests on its old, firm foundation; it offers to all who accept it the unchanging standards of Christ, the love of God and our neighbour in this life, and the sure hope of heaven in the next.

Is it not just this, perhaps, which makes the Marxist and the non-believing Existentialist so intolerably bitter with the Christian Faith? There is all the difference in the world between merely not knowing God: being, so to speak, unaware of Him, and their passionate, vivid refusal of him. One wonders sometimes if this latter can be called atheism at all in the ordinary sense of the word. It is so much more than a mere disbelief: it is a violent assertion of the utter impossibility of the existence of God. "The lady doth protest too much, methinks." Do not, in fact, the Marxist and the Existentialist betray, by the very hurling thunders of their denunciations and the agony of their disbelief, the presence of a terrible, haunting fear that God may be there after all: may be able to shatter to pieces at a word all the flimsy fabric of that make-believe-world-of-their-own which they have so boldly constructed from such unenduring material?

The growing paganism of our England of to-day—an England still so sunny and so sweet—is, needless to say, a very different affair to all this of which we have been thinking. It is almost entirely the negative form of atheism (except in the case of the Communists) or perhaps scarcely even so clear-cut a thing as that. Among intellectuals it may be, but among by far the larger number, it is surely still no more than an increasing carelessness about life in general, which necessarily includes religion, born partly of ignorance, and partly also of a great boredom and impatience with the teaching of most of the religious and political sects of which they have the choice. One has a certain sympathy with this attitude, and it is from just this that Catholics have to try and rescue them. A surprisingly large number of people will say, when talking quite honestly of their absence of religious belief: "Of course if I were anything I should be a Catholic." They are conscious of something in the Faith which is real; a good deal more real than positive atheism; of something unmistakably alive among so much in our poor world which is dead or dying.

It is just this atmosphere of brimming life and hope which every Catholic should bring others to share with him. But first of all, of course, he must possess it himself. Not every Catholic is a fount of brimming life and hope by any means. Apart from the personal joy of it, it is a great apostolate, for this much is certain. If one gets far enough away from the love of God one is, sooner or later, faced with the alternative of a philosophy of hate: Nietzsche, Marx, Hitler, Stalin. In Italy and France such a philosophy also has its exponents. Even in Britain we cannot hope to be exempt from it for ever unless we join in an active fight against it, and even now, one seems occasionally to perceive, against the far horizon, a figure which one day might come to be its living embodiment, as were those others.

No one can stand too much of this world without God, and that is a fact. Sooner or later disillusionment will fall upon us; we shall come to hate it and to hate the neighbour who, willynilly, shares it with us; that neighbour from whom we cannot get away. Sooner or later our trust in human nature will run the risk of being shattered, and the lurking figure of death, from which we have so long fled in imagination, come to meet us in the shadows of the falling night.

Only faith in God can lift us above human existence and give us the infinite peace, the infinite assurance, which make life, even on earth, worth while. For there is nothing on earth itself which can fully satisfy the human heart and the human understanding. That heart and that understanding were made ultimately for God and He alone can fill them.

CHAPTER VI

THE HOLY INNOCENTS

OR once Sister Imelda seemed a trifle ruffled. It was the Feast of the Holy Innocents and she had been in the parlour, a rare occurrence for her. She actually penetrated as far as the kitchen in order to tell me about it, for the Feast of the Holy Innocents is a very special feast in the novitiates of most religious orders, and on this day everyone appears to penetrate everywhere. But even when she reached me she could not talk to me about it, for we were already talking about fish. Unfortunately fish is not a commodity which keeps indefinitely and, I must say, ours seemed to be nearing the end of its tether. Anthony, who lay within the glow of the old-fashioned kitchen range in a state of semi-consciousness, induced I grieve to relate by over indulgence in the pleasures of the table, stirred uneasily at the oft-repeated word.

"Fish?" exclaimed Sister Imelda, uniting her voice to that of the First-in-the-Kitchen, "I thought I smelt it somewhere; I should say . . ."

"Don't," I implored, "because we have got to eat it in any case and it tastes so much better if it is not put into actual words."

"It is very nice fish I am sure," said the White Veil loyally.

Anthony could bear it no longer. He rose and staggered over to his empty dish. Nobody paid the slightest attention to him but he sat down hopefully beside it.

"Which plates are we to use for the first portion?" enquired the voice of an unaccustomed helper as she produced two from the cupboard.

"This one," interjected the First hastily, looking round to make sure that the provisor was not in sight, "it is a different shape, and it takes much less to fill it than the usual one." She had calculated without Sister Imelda, however, who was regarding her with profound reproach.

"But, Sister, it is a big feast, and the novices will be hungry; you forget, their plates inside will be the usual size."

The cup of innocent joy was full to the brim as far as I was concerned, and I felt that it only needed the presence of our postulant to make it overflow completely. And at that precise moment the cautious head of Sister Elizabeth did, in fact, appear round the edge of the door.

"May I come in?" she enquired in an anxious voice. We wreathed ourselves hastily in welcoming smiles, while the cat, who was once more stretched before the fire, rolled over on his back and waved all four legs in the air. "Hullo, Anthony," she said affably, "had a drop too much?"

I shuddered. The White Veils chuckled in unison. Sister Imelda looked at me and there was meaning in our eyes as they met. Behind the backs of the absorbed little group, we stole from the room.

"After all, it only happens once a year," she remarked charitably when at last we reached sanctuary.

"Thank God."

She sat down and smoothed out her scapular. "*Sponsa Christi is* all right, isn't it?" she asked abruptly.

"*Sponsa Christi* is very definitely all right. Why?"

"The Father in the parlour worried me a little. He

seemed almost to be making fun of it." I winced; I too had met that attitude.

"Some people make a practice of being funny about everything. Most of it is merely part of the modern pose. There is nothing humorous about *Sponsa Christi*, I promise you. What did he say?"

"Only that we should have to alter the shape of our habit now, and that we should have to get permission to go up to London and study the shop-windows to get the latest fashions for the new design, and foolish things like that. I did not like it." Her eyes were cloudy and puzzled, with a hurt look in them which somehow hurt me too.

"Just the English way of reacting to something big— never mind. When something big happens, we always pretend to think it humorous: national habit: don't let it worry you."

"But he is a religious, you know."

"He did not mean it."

"We are not really going to have to change, are we?"

"We are not going to have to change at all, provided that we have grasped our own vocation, and have realized its present-day setting. Of course, if we have not done that yet, then the sooner we do it the better. It is as simple as A.B.C. In the old days contemplatives could live on their revenues; they could also expect to get alms; bare necessities were cheap. They themselves probably had dowries between them, and there were plenty of good and benevolent people ready and anxious to help them to live. Don't you see that now all that is changed? The cost of even the barest living has risen incredibly all over the world. In most countries there are no rich people left, except those who ought not to be and who certainly would not give away any of it in alms. As for the dowries and securities of the nuns, they have mostly ceased to exist. You must remember that *Sponsa Christi* was written for nuns all over the world, not just for the British who are probably better off than almost any others."

She looked relieved.

"Added to that, the contemplative religious in England have always had to be more or less self-supporting. This is not a Catholic country, and even enclosed communities have had to earn their living as a matter of course. You don't need me to tell you all the things which nuns do to make money; all of them Catholic and most of them useful. It is only a matter now of making rather more in order to meet rising expenses." I was getting quite out of breath with my explanations; Sister Imelda even managed to smile.

"Vestments, altar-breads, Christmas cards, holy pictures, carvings, paintings of every sort—less said about most of them the better—copying manuscripts. There is no end to the holy activities of enclosed religious in this country. But one gathers that it has not been quite like that everywhere else, and the Holy Father only wishes to remind us that, although our vocation is just as necessary as it ever was, yet, as St. Paul and our Rule tell us, 'if any man will not work, neither let him eat.' I think he wants us to remember that, although our vocation is just as lovely as in days gone by, just as much at the heart of the Church and at his own paternal heart, yet we must not be hangers-on, 'parasites living on the Catholic community' as one very frank Father suggested to me. . . ."

"Horrible!" murmured Sister Imelda.

"Horrible to be it, but not so horrible to say it perhaps. After all, it is perfectly true. It is thoroughly unrealistic not to grasp that anyone, to pull his own weight nowadays, must first take his weight off the community in general. There are plenty of people who, through no fault of their own, cannot do that, without enclosed religious to add to the number. The real sick, the genuinely old and decrepit, those whose minds have become unbalanced, orphans: all of these have to be cared for by the State or by charitable people. It would be disgraceful if perfectly able-bodied women, under the plea of practising a particular form of prayer, were to allow themselves to increase the number."

"Quite." Sister Imelda nodded profound agreement. "And in a way the same thing spiritually, I suppose?" I nodded back.

"Well, yes. If we have to recognize the changed economic circumstances in which we follow our vocation, I suppose we have also to recognize that the spiritual aspect of the vocation has changed too. The Holy Father makes that equally clear. What used to be almost entirely a personal matter—a call to practise a certain type of prayer which was congenial to a certain type of soul; a call to lose touch with the world in which we live in order to get into closer touch with the world of the spirit—has now become an apostolate."

I thought that sounded rather nice, and most encouraging, but Sister Imelda, I noticed, shuddered slightly.

"Horrible word," she murmured, "I never really quite know what it means?"

"Neither did I," I admitted, "until I looked it up in the dictionary the other day. It means 'Leadership in a propaganda'."

"Propaganda!" moaned Sister Imelda, suddenly suffering a severe relapse, "that's just what *he* said; that *Sponsa Christi* was only another piece of propaganda. Oh, why wasn't I born a hundred years ago?"

"You were, very nearly," I said hastily, but perhaps tactlessly as I realized a moment too late. Fortunately

she shot right over the remark in pursuit of her subject.

"Apostles—apostolates—propaganda—no, no, no. . . ."
She groaned aloud. "At our age. . . ."

I began to wish that I had not placed her at quite so
near a hundred: a wicked libel too, I reflected, seeing
that she had not yet reached her three score years and
ten. Strange how differently things sound when one is
saying them oneself, and when they are being said, particularly if one is inadvertently included where one had
not meant to be.

"Of course you are a great deal younger than I am,"
she conceded, looking at me forlornly. I found no comfort in the thought, after all, if it made her feel lonely.

"Now look here, Sister," I said kindly but firmly, "let
us pull ourselves together." I determined that at least
she should not be alone in tact and delicacy. "They
are horrible words, every one of them, I admit. But all
they really mean is this: that it is our work as nuns to
bring the fact of Christ home to the world which is
ignoring Him, just as the apostles travelled everywhere
preaching Christ's resurrection to the nation which had
crucified Him, and to Gentiles who had never even heard
His name. In other words, our religious outlook must
become enlarged beyond the individual and circum-
scribed little orbit of our own spiritual welfare—although of course we must never presume to lose sight
of that altogether—to include instead the spiritual welfare of the whole earth."

I felt like one of the banished books down in the
carpentering shed, so sententious I sounded, but under
the soothing influence of the long words, Sister Imelda
appeared to revive a little; her usual buoyancy of manner
began to return.

"Human things and spiritual things are so mixed

up," she agreed with a shake of the head, "one can't disentangle them. That is quite true. But surely the natural ought to adapt itself to the spiritual and not the other way round?" Then she shook her head again even more decidedly. "No, I am wrong; of course I am wrong. God came down from heaven to save the earth; He did not lift the earth up to heaven. He took the human way to show us what He meant; He followed our manner of living; He adapted Himself to His own gene-ration of men. In any case I am not sure that it is per-fectly wise even to wish to isolate oneself from the human as they used to do in the desert. It suited their tem-perament, but"—Sister Imelda lowered her voice dis-creetly—"I am not so sure about nowaday temperaments. It seems to me that sometimes when they get too far in-side themselves, they open the wrong door: not the one marked God but the one marked Self." There was a knock outside.

"Oh, dear," sighed Sister Imelda, "Holy Innocents again. This time they've found the one marked You."

"Well, let us adapt ourselves to the Holy Innocents then," said I, and pulled back the door with a flourish, whereupon the whole lot of them fell headlong into the room at once. The adaptations proceeded, but not perhaps altogether according to schedule. They seemed a somewhat gayer affair than the books led one to sup-pose. But then, of course, the writers were not thinking specifically of the Feast of the Holy Innocents which only happens once a year.

When at last they had gone, my thoughts returned to Sister Imelda. It is true that this intermingling of spiritual and human issues in life is one of the things from which there seems no escape. Even if we imagine that we can separate the two sufficiently, in any given case, to be able to say decidedly, "this is human, that is

E

spiritual," we shall nearly always find that the fact or experience of which we are speaking has at least its counterpart on the other plane.

Take, for instance, the interest and pleasure aroused by the ordinary human experiences of friendship and career. In the case of two friends, they may often disagree over trifling matters. One may want to go for a walk and the other to stay indoors; one may prefer this book, the other that; they may argue quite vehemently over the points; they may even squabble. Yet the foundations of the friendship are as steady and safe as foundations can be. There exists a mutual respect and liking, a fundamental agreement upon essential principles and major preferences. which leaves the structure of the friendship unshaken by momentary differences of surface opinions.

In the same way, some work undertaken, some profession adopted, may at times tax our patience to the limit: music, for instance, or art, or science, or anything else which requires prolonged and steady application: yet the pursuer would never really hesitate as to going on.

When a breakdown therefore occurs in any such case, it would seem that it occurs because of an essential, and not merely exterior, defect in the friend or the profession, or because of an essential and not merely exterior defect on the part of the first person concerned. In other words, when we really collapse and finally give up anyone or anything, it is usually either because we have discovered that they were not all that we thought them, or, contrarywise, have discovered that we were not, by any means, all that we thought ourselves!

Now to take this experience on the spiritual plane, in following a religious vocation the same process may occur. A novice may discover that the life is, after all, not sufficiently inspiring, as far as she is concerned, to hold her attention and her whole endeavour for life. It need hardly be stressed how important it is to discover, in this case, just as in the equivalent case in the world, whether the flaw lies in her or in the life itself.

If it lies in the life itself, if this is not really in conformity with the ideal and the ultimate aim of the young religious, undoubtedly she will be right to go—not back to the world permanently, but back to the search for her ideal, in so far as that can ever be found on earth. (But incidentally we must not forget that, in its completeness, it is never to be found on earth.) If, on the other hand, the flaw is in the character of the person concerned, a valiant fight may yet set the trouble right.

Yet how are we to know which it is? Not by our own judgment, that is certain, and therein lies our great difficulty, for it is probably by our own judgment that we shall wish to be guided at this early stage of the religious life. Yet our own judgment, under the stress of difficult circumstances, is not reliable.

A minor test of sincerity may indeed be just the very simple one mentioned above. Is it to the world that we wish to return, or is it merely that we wish to serve God in some other religious environment? Yet even that is not altogether a safe indication of the sincerity of our protests that *this* is not what we were looking for. It may not be; nevertheless it is still just possible that it was what God was offering us. Cases have been known where a disgruntled postulant or novice returned to the world intending to enter some other, and more ideal, Order, and instead found herself back in the world for ever. Either each fresh essay ended in the same headlong flight, or fresh essays were only made on paper and never materialized.

In all such cases, time is the real safety. If an aspirant will wait patiently until the six months of her probation are over, and then say, firmly and decidedly, that she does not feel the call of God to such a way of life, we may be fairly happily assured that she is right; and the same applies to any novice who will wait her full canonical year before making the final decision. The very last thing which the devil wants, one may be sure, is patience, thought, slow consideration. Yet, after all, if we had honestly meant to give all our life to God, as we did, it is not very much to give Him one year out of it, just to be quite sure that we are not making a mistake in leaving His service.

There is, however, one pitfall which it is as well to avoid for the sake of all concerned. It is that of a sudden decision to go forward, just before any definite step in the religious life, where there had previously been marked hesitation and indecision. One must beware of those who abruptly change their minds at such a moment. Most probably they will change them again immediately after. Unconsciously it is the sudden prospect of a little break and excitement; the pleasure of the prospective congratulations of friends; the feeling of having achieved something definite in the eyes of the world and of one's own family circle; the fact, even in the convent, of being for the moment an object of attention in what seem to us the highest circles, which is causing the momentary enthusiasm. The decision to lead a hard life for God is not reached by such exterior and accidental inducements.

Prayer, quiet determination, a resolution to embrace suffering should suffering come, and to persevere to the end along a stony path for the love of God—these are the old and well-tried ways which bring us through the difficult days of our novitiate, and indeed will serve us until the day of our death. There is no short-cut to religious perfection nor, for the matter of that, any new method of attaining to sudden sanctity. The grace of God, our own endeavours and failures, our perseverance in face of the latter, and the occasional successes which serve to hearten us—these have to suffice.

But if the weakness of purpose lies in our own character, and not in any real falling-short in the Order to which we have been called, ah, then it is worth while indeed to make one desperate effort to lift ourselves above ourselves, catch at the outstretched hand of God, and so remain above our poor, weak, human possibilities for ever. The present or—for ever. That is our choice: and how many have chosen the present! Let us allow ourselves instead to be captured by the thought of that 'for ever'. For ever to have earned the privilege of serving God and loving Him supremely and, by some incomprehensible, divine generosity of His, just because we gave our miserable little 'present' on earth, which was all that we had to give, to be given in return an eternity of His love; love such as we cannot dream. Just this one moment of time that we are living to-day is ours. We can pull it towards ourselves, or—even though it be done with tears and averted head—we can push it towards God. He will accept it, be it never so poor, never so shabbily given.

CHAPTER VII

FEAR

A PRIEST was talking to me in the parlour one day and I happened to ask him what he considered the dominant note of the mentality of this generation. "Fear," he replied, without a moment's hesitation. I own I was startled. "I did not say cowardice," he added with a little laugh.

I tested the idea on my next encounter with the twenties in the parlour.

"Priscilla," I said abruptly and without any attempt at a useless finesse, "are you ever afraid?"

"Rather!" replied Priscilla with engaging candour. "What of?"

"War." She paused and I waited. "You see," she said simply, "if Peter had to go. . . ."

I wondered what the point of view of the Peters of the world might be, so I asked the young brother of one of our sisters on his next visit. There is nothing like getting one's information direct from the source. He is still an undergraduate and I tried it, I hope, more tactfully this time.

"Are you ever afraid of *anything*, Tommy?" I enquired respectfully.

"Afraid?" He hesitated. "Well, no, not afraid; why should one be?" I did not say any more and he considered the proposition for a moment or two in silence. "Certainly not afraid; but I'll tell you what, I often feel sort of frustrated if that's what you mean?" He paused again. "No one knows what's going to happen next; sometimes one feels a kind of block—one can't get *on* with life. One can never look far enough ahead, because one is always coming up against an 'if', and then another 'if'." He spoke quite gravely, without a trace of petulance or resentment. "Was life always just a series of 'ifs'?" he asked. I, too, considered the point.

"No," I said at last. "I think it used to be much more a series of 'whens'. When this—when that. That was before the war, Tommy, when you were a small boy."

"I see." I heard the scraping of his chair as he pushed it back and got up to go. "That would be nice," he said politely, "I think I wish it were still before the war."

"It is," I replied a little grimly, and with that he went out again into his world of 'ifs', and I slipped back into the comforting atmosphere of God and His 'when'. For with God there is never an 'if', nor could be.

Obviously a state of more or less habitual fear leads, according to temperament, to two attitudes of mind—naturally speaking, that is. Recklessness or apathy.

"If life is uncertain, then let us at least enjoy it while it lasts; and since it is so uncertain, it is of no great use to take elaborate precautions about anything. Let us just get on with what is nearest at hand without worrying about to-morrow. The main thing is to enjoy ourselves, to live, while we can." Or again: "What is the use of making any great effort when the world may be blown to bits to-morrow? One must go on living, of course, until it is, but what is the use of making plans, or trying to do anything worth while? One cannot avert whatever is going to happen; it has got beyond us; the only thing is to sit down and wait for it and hope that it will soon be over when it comes."

Neither of these points of view is going to get us very far, that is certain. It is unnecessary to labour the obvious fact that fear plays havoc with any army, and it is as part of an army that all practising Christians are bound to regard themselves to-day, if they are to think logically or coherently about religion at all. It is a case of conscription, and it is of no use to waste time in grumbling when that occurs. One just goes.

Perhaps the shortest cut to the avoidance of mental fear is sincerity. Nothing is too bad to be borne if one faces it squarely. It is the running away, the half hoping, the trying not to think, all the camouflages and subterfuges, which wear us out in reality, and not the actual object of the fear in itself. Usually we never get so far as coming to grips with the true object because we are so feverishly trying to persuade ourselves that it is not there. It is well known, of course, that nothing lends itself so easily to disguise as fear.

If, for instance, a person is being absurdly nervous and what might be called "fussy" about trifles such as locking up at night, shutting windows, turning out lights, and so on, it is often no more than a sign that they have a constant and wearing anxiety, deep down in their consciousness. They will go back, and back again, to make sure that they have really turned that key, or put out that electric light, and be no more satisfied the third time than they were the first. All these exterior trifles are quite simply so many camouflages for the big worry which they are unable to resolve in their own mind. Were that to be satisfactorily dealt with, the minor anxieties would disappear automatically.

Something of the same kind is true of pain, the twin sister in suffering of anxiety. As we know in the case of physical pain, what makes it bearable is when it takes the forms of spasms which pass; when there is occasional respite. The same is true of spiritual and mental pain. We learn in time that it does not endure without pause;

it comes and goes; increases and again eases. That is so not only in the case of incidental spiritual pain but, in a larger sense, of the whole pain of life, that indescribable *weltschmerz* which some of us know so well. If we come to regard it as no more than a solitary spasm in an eternal existence (and, considered in proportion, it is no more) we shall not only survive it but even be quite cheerful about it. One can always bear life as a part of eternity.

Yet one thing is certain: if we are going to be really sincere with ourselves and with others, the first essential is to be sincere with God. That is, as a matter of fact, a completely absurd expression since, however much we might try, we can none of us be anything else when it comes to the point. It is, however, the kind of expression which is commonly used.

"It is so difficult to be honest and straightforward even with God!" has sighed many a worthy but mistaken beginner in the spiritual life. It is impossible to be anything else—He being God; but they have not yet found that out. In one sense it does not matter in the least what we explain to God about ourselves and our affairs, since He knows every vibration of our being, and every thought in our head, without requiring us to tell Him—or to lie to Him—about it. Ordinarily speaking, perhaps, the less we explain ourselves to God the better: it is, to say the least of it, so very superfluous. Adam and Eve hid themselves among the trees of paradise in the cool of the evening, we may remember; but it was not a very successful concealment.

In the spiritual life—that is, in any life lived for God, whether active or contemplative—this matter of self-deception and delusion is constantly cropping up and has been written about *ad nauseam*. But it is so fundamental a matter that it is almost impossible not to come back to it, and it has a particular bearing on this question of fear, since self-deception and posing are one of the commonest means of escape from it. People run away from a reality which terrifies them and may, if they are not careful, run straight into that soul-stifling world of dreams which waits for any of us round the corner, if we are foolish enough in our panic to turn in that direction.

Now playing happily with fancies to ease the tension of our minds might not matter much for a time if it remained at that, but unfortunately it rarely does remain at that. Almost inevitably the mental outlook gradually becomes more and more estranged from reality. Ultimately the dreamers will come to have a completely different view of life and of themselves from that of the people around them, and this disagreement finally develops into acute dissatisfaction on their side. They become aggrieved. The dissatisfaction is not with their dreams, but with the reaction of others to them.

From the point of view of doing anything useful for the world, such souls are, to say the least of it, putting themselves at an enormous disadvantage. Actually, they are sick souls and need help. At some stage or other, if the mischief is not checked, they will almost certainly find it necessary to begin to impose their fancies on their neighbours, since these latter will not voluntarily accept them and, to do this effectually, the help of outside events has to be called in. They must have tangible evidence, and the evidence is usually of such a dramatic nature as to be very trying for those who live with them. Sometimes imaginary illnesses develop which it is extraordinarily difficult to disentangle from the reality; sometimes strange happenings take place, and increase and multiply, to the acute discomfort of their friends. It is to be noticed that votive lamps which they light almost invariably blow up. They know by mystic insight what other people are thinking and doing, and are very upset indeed when they find out that they are wrong. So, of course, are the other people. They have an unfortunate habit of falling downstairs and off their bicycles, which catastrophes they attribute directly to the intervention of the devil, and refuse all normal explanations with a pitying sorrow for our blindness, and a grudging acceptance of our sticking-plaster.

Now it is true that all these things can really happen to the saints—but with a difference. In the first place, it is not the saints who draw attention to them but other people who do the noticing and the talking. If the saints are told that their adventures are imaginary, they take it very placidly. Probably they very heartily wish that they were. Not having produced the adventures but only having suffered from them, they are not in the least interested in their effect on other people. The difficulty with a saint is to persuade him that he is not a great sinner, and perfectly ordinary at that: the difficulty with a neurotic of this type is to persuade her that she is.

If we are to avoid fear under all its disguises let us give up any lingering dreams, and turn round and boldly face our mental bogeys. Probably most of us have them. There is, for instance, fear of the possibility of the use of the hydrogen bomb, or again the accidental destruction of the world by some atomic explosion. Gabriel Marcel tells us that such fears exist. "What is clear," he remarks, "is that to-day men are in the presence of a fact which could not have been conceived as possible at the beginning of the century; they know that it is in their power to destroy the universe."

Now if that were true, people with weak nerves might be forgiven for abandoning themselves to despair and terror. But fortunately it is not. Gabriel Marcel may be a profound philosopher as far as Existentialism is concerned, but with all due respect to his learning, he is surely over-estimating the extent of human power. God created the universe, and God will bring it to an end at His own moment; but it is quite certain that no one else will. God can use any instrument He chooses to achieve His ends, or to punish His children when they become too outrageous; as He used floods, and pestilence, and the conquering kings of neighbouring lands in the olden days. But God's universe remains His own, and we could no more destroy it than we could have made it originally, or have kept it in repair all down the ages.

We cannot even keep our own houses in repair without immense fuss and many licences, and it is likely that we could manage to maintain the universe in its smooth and silent working day and night, and the perfection of its constant, yet almost invisible renewal? Where should we find batteries to feed the light of the stars? From whence get the inexhaustible petrol that keeps the sun for ever rotating upon its axis? Who would drive the engine which first set our earth spinning in the air, yet holds it in perfect equilibrium while it revolves slowly round the sun? Philosophers are very wonderful people, there is no doubt of that: but then, so are the flies on the wheel—from the point of view of the flies.

Once, a very long time ago, men thought that they could build a tower which would reach up to heaven. They thought that they were very remarkable people because they had actually learnt how to make bricks. Now if they could make bricks, they could obviously build a tower up to heaven with them; and if we can make a hydrogen bomb, then of course we can blow up the universe with it.

The answer may be that although bricks and bombs belong to man, neither heaven nor the universe does.

They happen to belong to Someone Else. So, for a long time, God watched the little men running about very busy with their building, as He is now watching all our activities with bombs and other things. And then He came quietly down from that heaven of His, and with one push sent everything flying, as a push sends flying a child's house of cards.

"'They have begun to do this,' said God, 'neither will they leave off from their designs till they accomplish them in deed. Come ye, therefore, let us go down. . . .' And so the Lord scattered them from that place into all lands, and they ceased to build the city."

Now what God smashed at Babel was not so much the tower, which would have been unlikely to become a serious danger to heaven in any case, but the presumption of the idea of those foolish children. Wherever we see presumption among men, we can be quite sure in our minds of the ultimate effect upon God. He will not have it. He stands it for a long while, and He lets us make fools of ourselves to our hearts' content, in the hope that we shall see the error of our ways. But if we do not: if He is obliged to remark: "This is but the beginning of their undertakings, and what is to prevent them carrying out all they design?" then we may be sure that, sooner or later, He will also add: "It would be well to go down. . . ." And that is the end of our towers which reach to heaven, and our hydrogen bombs which blow up the universe, and all the follies and presumptions of men. We may perhaps be allowed to wreck our own affairs but we must leave God's affairs alone.

We have no need to be afraid so long as God is in heaven and we believe in Him. Even Browning knew that. Man has invented explosives, and he is confident that, so far as they are concerned, he can control them. What he fears that he cannot control are the other men who may use them. But God made the other men. If we can control the bombs which we have made, cannot God control the men whom He has made? We can trust Him to see that they do not destroy His universe, until the moment comes which He has fixed for its passing, and that passing will be according to His design and not according to ours. It is not man who can destroy God's work, but only God Himself. We have no one to be afraid of but Himself, and He is a merciful God to those who love and worship Him.

The Christian, by the mere fact of being a Christian, can act as such a steadying influence in the world if only he will! People everywhere are trying to adapt themselves to an impossible situation, to live harmoniously amid violently explosive circumstances. It really cannot be done. But the Christian can do something much better. We have already spoken of the value and the comfort of those people who adapt themselves readily to any situation and manage to fit in anywhere. Sooner or later they begin to command that situation whatever it is; others look to them for a lead; turn to them to know what to do next.

Now the final and the only really useful adaptation of man is to the will of God, and that is precisely the supreme adaptation which the Christian can show to the world. For the Christian fits easily into an universe which he never for a moment imagines to be his own, and co-operates readily with designs which he never for a moment supposes that he originated. There is no fear in his soul, because he happens to know the Owner of the Universe in which he lives, and he is aware, although perhaps a little dimly as befits his station, of the supreme beauty of the design which it is his destiny to help carry out. He is humbly pleased to do his small allotted share, and he has complete confidence that everything

has been planned with perfect wisdom, and that ultimately it will work out exactly as it was intended.

It may include Towers of Babel, and hydrogen bombs,
and even worse things than those but, when all is said and
done, such inventions are no more than children's toys
in the eyes of God. And that is the end of the Christian's
fear.

CHAPTER VIII

UNCHANGING EVE

SISTER Imelda and I were discussing Adam and Eve;
the fact is, we have never agreed about them. We
are agreed about the story in Genesis, needless to
say, but it is when it comes to what is written between
the lines that we do not quite see eye to eye. What is
written between the lines will always interest a woman
more than just the part which is printed, because a
woman always wants to know *why*. Which is, after all,
no more than Eve did. We began, therefore, by speaking of curiosity, a womanly quality upon which Sister
Imelda counts absolutely, although singularly devoid of
it herself.

"It is no good hiding your head in the sand like an
ostrich; curiosity is there, and it is better to reckon
with it." She lowered her voice confidentially. "To
tell the truth, we have been like that ever since Eve.
She started it." I was glad to receive this inside information, so to speak, and nodded my head knowingly.

"Why," said I, with deep interest, in case she had
any inside information on that point also, "does charm
count so much more than intellect?"

"With Adam you mean? Because God put consciousness of Eve's charm so deep in Adam's heart that he
couldn't get away from it. You see He *had* to. If it
hadn't been so deep in Adam, how could he ever have
forgiven her after she had spoilt his beautiful world for
him?" I stared.

"I never thought of that! No, I never did!" I said reflectively. "And how many worlds has Eve not spoilt for Adam since—and been forgiven! I never thought of that either."

"If he had not admired Eve so much he could never have forgiven what she had done. And it wasn't exactly intellect which she displayed over the serpent, was it? Poor Adam. He would just have gone away, and sat down in a corner of Eden, and bowed his head and died, and that would have been the end of it." There was no doubt as to where Sister Imelda's sympathies lay. "And that *couldn't* be the end of it, because God wanted His world to go on, and them to give good example to all the generations which came after them."

"I don't know that it was such a very *good* example?" I said doubtfully.

"Oh, *yes*! Why, they stayed together and were excellent friends for nine hundred years, and never even thought of the word divorce. . . ."

I find Sister Imelda's theological instructions a little startling at times perhaps, but all the same one has a queer feeling that they are fundamentally sound.

"Do you remember," she went on, looking past me out into the courtyard where the February sun threw pale yellow splashes on the uneven cobbles, "that sailor-captain whom we were told about a long time ago, who was wrecked in the Atlantic, and refused to leave his ship, and was days alone on it, hundreds of miles from shore?"

I was counting up the number of different shades of brown which there are in a late winter garden. Grey, mostly, is just grey, with two or three tones of it only, all equally grey; but brown will range from an almost crimson tint to the first beginnings of the delicious yellow of spring. Even in the small space beyond me, enclosed

F

in the arched circle of the door, I could count the terra-
cotta brown of syringa stems, the purplish-brown shoots
of a wild rose, and the more deeply purple earth of a
burnt-out bonfire. Beyond that again was the plain
brown of an old apple tree against the wall, with the
warm, weathered brown of its tiles at the top; and, beside that, the mauvey-brown of dead goldenrod stalks
and the yellow-brown haze of Michaelmas daisies. I
wondered why she had suddenly switched from the
Garden of Eden to the middle of the Atlantic, only
to find, as I so often do, that she had not switched at
all.

"Well, we heard all about him, didn't we? We could
not help hearing about him three or four times a day,
as if he were really there. We here, enclosed and double-
enclosed in Puddleshire, and he in the middle of the
ocean, and feeling as if he were our brother; people
coming into the chapel all day long and asking prayers
that the tow-rope would not break again, or that the
ship would not turn turtle before he could jump clear.
Don't you see that God is preparing us to go back to the
old days of the Garden of Eden? Just one big family.
Adam and Eve with all their children, and the animals
wandering round them everywhere? When one of the
little beasties in the Zoo becomes ill nowadays, all the
world is told immediately, and they fly bamboo-shoots
or rice, or whatever is specially required, across to it
from the country where it came from. The human
family has grown since those first days; spread all over the
earth; the Garden of Eden has become the wide world.
Soon we shall all be brothers and sisters again with God,
our Father, walking among us in the cool of the evening."

The charm of the picture mingled with the spring
sunshine, and lingered on our little corner of the earth

at least, in that way which is the secret of Sister Imelda.

"May one ask . . . how long, do you think?"

"I hope that you and I will both live to see it," replied Sister Imelda with great decision, and continued to saw up small lengths of wood. Evidently she was not going to allow herself to be disturbed by the prospect. She handed me the seccotine with equal firmness and I began meekly to stick them together, two by two. I own to feeling a little overwhelmed and weakish at the thought of the immediate advent of all this. But certainly, when one comes to consider it, as far as Adam and Eve are concerned, we do not seem to have changed crucially since the early days. Judging by the information given in what sister Imelda darkly calls 'those books', Eve is still Eve, although within a convent wall.

"What do you *really* think about Eve, Sister?" I asked in a whisper, after a pause. Sister Imelda looked round to make sure that no one else was listening, and that there was nothing in the least resembling a snake in sight. After all, there is a certain loyalty to one's own sex.

"*Horrid.* Nasty little thing," she said, under her breath, "but that is only between you and me."

At that moment our latest edition of Eve appeared round the corner; then, catching sight of us, made as if to turn back. I beckoned her to approach.

"Have you by chance any ideas on the subject of Eve?" I enquired, anxious to make her feel at home in what, after all, we wish her to regard as a sort of modern Garden of Eden.

"Oh, yes. Lots. Doubt if you would approve of them." I tried hastily to change the subject, but Sister Imelda, alert as always to correct error should any be present, hung on like a bulldog.

"You," she remarked severely, "would probably not

have made aprons at all, instead you would have wished to go in for the modern fashion. . . ."

"Slacks," finished Sister Elizabeth placidly. "Oh, yes."

I became aware, as I so often have before, of the need of a new kind of sign in conversation-punctuation. Each punctuation-mark has its counterpart in voice-inflection, but there is need for a simple mark, in both departments, to express the act of ignoring. There is a sign for a question, for an exclamation, for a pause: but where is the sign for that complete stone-deafness and wall-eyedness which it is only fitting should at times come over us?

An inverted interrogation-mark might serve the purpose in writing, but what can one do in speaking to mark one's emotions? A long silence is totally inadequate— particularly as the less sensitive are almost certain to think that one merely has not heard. However, on this occasion I stared before me with such an exceedingly glassy expression, that even Sister Imelda became aware of something wrong and hastened to the rescue.

"Now if I wore slacks," she said affably, sitting as it were on the conversational fence between us and obviously without the vaguest idea of what was the matter, "I should also put on a sacking apron in front and another at the back. . . ." Sister Elizabeth gave it up; she dropped her head into her hands and rocked gently.

"Probably," continued Sister Imelda, still intent on appeasement and tact, "there were faults on both sides; there usually are. Now that does not matter at all, provided the faults are faults of human weakness and not of principle. If people have the same interior standard; if they follow the same ideal, and sense of duty, and have the same desires and *mean* them; it does not matter if occasionally they have to watch each other fail and fall afterwards. It does not irritate or disappoint in the same way. It is quite a different matter to watching identical conduct, done not by mere human frailty, but because it is regarded as right. One is due to momentary weakness, the other to wrong principles, or lack of all principle. Adam and Eve never said afterwards that they had been right—although they did try to excuse themselves by blaming the devil and each other. But, after all, the more they blamed, the more they showed that they knew they had been wrong."

" Where *do* you get your ideas from? I wish I knew on what principles you do your thinking? " said Sister Elizabeth, still smiling.

"It is very simple," replied Sister Imelda innocently, "it is like a sort of machine in one's head; it works by itself. I just put in two ideas at one end, and what I think comes out at the other.'

"What do you do on the days when you have not got even two ideas? "

"Cut one in half, of course," said I.

"Oh, I see," agreed Sister Elizabeth blankly, but Sister Imelda looked faintly shocked. Such days, one feels, do not occur in her case.

"The great thing in thinking, if you want your thinking to be clear," she continued kindly, " is never to use a medium of expression in which you do not think naturally. Somebody once asked me to write a hymn for them, but I could not write a hymn because I do not think in hymns."

"Nor me," said the postulant sympathetically. We hardly, perhaps, needed to be told.

"Some people think in colour, some in sound, some in ink. A real gardener, for instance, thinks in colour, in form, even in scent—but not in sound or ink, why should he? "

"Oh, no."

"It is exactly the same supernaturally. Some think spiritually in charity, some in truth, some in humanity, some in active zeal: as many shades of difference as there are virtues, and intensities of virtue."

"She talks just like a book, doesn't she," said the postulant admiringly, "at least some books. Not like the books on religious novitiates which I read just before I entered. . . ."

Unconsciously Sister Imelda and I both stiffened; we stared at each other and the same ghastly suspicion shone in our eyes. I do not honestly think that it had occurred to either of us before, that of course would-be postulants could read those books just as well as we could. They were on sale for all to buy. Of what use to banish them to the carpentering-shed and use them mainly for pressing Christmas cards?

"They very nearly put me off entering altogether," continued Sister Elizabeth sweetly, "until I remembered that, after all, they were mainly written by men. This life, you see, is so different for them."

Sister Imelda gurgled helplessly in reply; her eyes were still starting from her head in alarm as she surveyed her latest ewe-lamb.

"Now, I ask you, could a man ever really know what it feels like *never* to have a holiday and *never* to have a change? He thinks he does, of course, because he has talked to a few nuns who never have a holiday and never have a change, and they have given him their best-Sunday-go-to-meeting reactions. But you have got *to* do it to know what it feels like." There was a certain grimness in her tone.

"Dear, dear," said Sister Imelda nervously, for all the world like a foster-hen watching her ducklings nearing the water for the first time, "don't let's think about it."

"Perhaps when I have been inside for fifty years I shall not think about it, or shall think about it as you do."

Sister Imelda looked at her shrewdly. "Not if you spend the next fifty years in wanting a holiday, my child," she said. "You will have to get the beginning right first if you want the end to be."

"Tell me why the books put you off?" I asked quietly.

"Well. . . ."

"Was it that you thought the people inside queer?"

"Good heavens, no," said Sister Elizabeth genuinely enough. "It was not the queer people inside, but the queer people outside who wanted to get in, who worried me! Suffering from every sort of neurosis, according to one book, and being dealt with by their novice-mistresses for troubled minds. It suggested that their confidence had to be won, like mice with a bit of cheese, and they were encouraged to talk like half-loonies in front of a psychiatrist. It actually said in one chapter, I remember, that however wise and skilful the superior might be, there would occasionally be sisters who would defeat even her. The *victim*—that word very nearly finished me—the victim, in spite of all which the superior could do, remained distressed, unhappy, strange in her behaviour. I hated it."

"I hadn't seen that bit," said Sister Imelda looking at me solemnly, "I really hadn't."

"You haven't seen a lot of bits,' I replied shortly, "I stuck the pages together."

"If you were to read the parts about anxiety-neurosis and anxiety-state," continued Sister Elizabeth, addressing Sister Imelda and now thoroughly enjoying herself, "you would simply swoon. Do you know what the symptoms in the wretched victims are—or may be? I'll tell you!" She was positively gloating over us in the most unseemly way. She reminded me of the Fat Boy in Pick-wick: "I wants to make your flesh creep."

"Palpitation; lack of appetite; or, contrariwise, full-ness in the—well, the *estomac*; weakness of limbs blurr-ing of vision; tinnitus. . . ."

"Sister Elizabeth, be quiet at once," said I, laughing.

"Well, then, may I give her just one more reassuring bit to end up with?" I nodded. "There are degrees, Sister, there are degrees. We don't get there all at once. You will be glad to know that there is a great difference between psychoses and psychoneuroses. The psychoses are the things really to avoid because they may com-pletely mislead the intellectual powers—if there are any intellectual powers to mislead, which seems unlikely. Now the psychoneuroses do not. You needn't go batty because you have a psychoneurosis, so I banked on that, and here I am." She smiled upon us largely. I got up.

"Sister Elizabeth, you are now busy in the altar-bread office, and I am busy doing accounts, and Sister Imelda is busy getting over her swoon. Good-bye." I watched her depart, then slowly followed along the path. As I went, I pulled out a letter which had come the day before from Rome, and glanced again at the words at the bottom of the page.

"P.S. Has your nice postulant an unconscious trick of raising her eyes suddenly and then looking down again without a word?—rather remarkable eyes by the way. And does she say 'Oh, yes,' and 'Oh, no,' to what-ever you ask her? or if, by accident, she makes a longer speech, does she blush very prettily, and then shut down the lid abruptly like a Jack-in-the-Box? If so, tell her I said that Mass for her; and tell her, please, to go on pray-ing for me."

"She does indeed to do all those things," I murmured to the empty air, and I do not know why, but I sighed a little. Perhaps I was thinking of Rome. There was a wall which ran down the hill sharply into the Via Sistina: a yellow-ochre wall, six or seven feet high, over the top of which there used to drift the scent of orange-blossom —overpowering, sweet. If I gave her the message it was to be hoped that she would not begin to think of things like that. But of course she would. Who could think of Rome and not remember its loveliness? The pale, English sunlight still fell in patches across the path where I stood. It was doing its best: no need to draw attention to its thin chilliness by unnecessary contrasts. The message from Rome, I decided, could wait a little.

CHAPTER IX

THE GREAT ABSURD

IF we accept the fact that sub-conscious fear plays a large part in the mental and emotional equipment of to-day, we must also bear in mind that fear has two sides to it: there is fear of life and fear of death. The two are entwined, but they are not quite the same fear. What one can certainly admire about this generation is its courage in the face of alarm, from whichever side the alarm comes.

If we trace it to its source, at the very back of fear, there nearly always lies the thought of death: the death of a loved person, the death of a hope, the death of ourselves. Were our earthly life everlasting, fear would surely disappear to a large extent, for in the everlasting nothing can be final, and finality is the thing we dread. We have lost some friend, or some possession, for ever: we shall miss what we believe to be our only chance in some matter vital to our happiness, and there will be no possibility of its recurring in our short lifetime.

Always, as it were, behind us, we hear the hurrying feet of death; always at the back of our mind is the knowledge that at some moment he will overtake us, or overtake one whom we love, and our earthly hopes, and our dreams, and our opportunities, will vanish alike into the engulfing past. Only belief in God and in heaven can save us permanently from such forebodings.

Plato believed in the immortality of the soul: Epicurus did not. The quarrel is as old as that, and still their descendants argue the same theme. Kierkegaard, Jaspers, Gabriel Marcel: Nietzsche, Heidegger, Sartre. The Neo-stoicism of Heidegger still beats against the sense of eternity so finely expressed by Kierkegaard in spite of the latter's manifest unorthodoxy. But these intricacies have no great interest for ordinary people like ourselves. "Men," Pascal tells us, "not having been able to cure death, misery and ignorance, have decided, in order to be happy, not to think about them."

Ordinary people, Régis Jolivet suggests, recognize no medium, when faced by the doctrine of Nihilism, between despair and a wild escape from the thought by means of distractions. Of the two, without the help of Faith, despair usually gains the day, since mere distraction is not sufficient to drown misery permanently. Epicurus is reported by Diogenes to have declared that, in relation to ourselves, death is really non-existent, because, if *we* exist it is not here yet: if *it* exists we are no longer there. That is the sort of thing which philosophers like to amuse themselves by saying, while, in the meantime, the rest of us try to grapple with events. It may have consoled Epicurus, but it is not in the least likely to console the ordinary person who has to live in the world as it is, and face death as it is, and cannot exist in a dreamy and speculative world of metaphysics.

This much, however, is certain: on the view we take of death depends the view we take of life, and a clear view in the soul on death is the only basis for a clear view of life. It will be generally found that those who consciously or unconsciously evade the problem of death, are inclined also to evade the problems of life and to live on the surface of existence. Now, living on the surface of anything spiritual is no sort of state for a Christian; it is better to turn round and face the whole of our destiny: the now and the hereafter.

There is often a muddled attitude, which can even be disastrous, as to the inter-relation of life and death. Religion half-understood seems little more support than no religion at all. What, one may be tempted to reflect, is the use of a religion which does not even succeed in making us understand that the earth is a time of probation; that suffering is an integral part of it; and that Christ's sufferings are meant to teach us how to bear our own? Let us get our Faith clear: faith in God, faith in heaven: and that will give us a solid and comforting faith in earth as the only means to the end.

The new conditions under which we live in this latter half of the twentieth century tend greatly to emphasize the fragility of the human being, and thus also the idea of the melancholy of existence. Indeed this sense of vulnerability is sufficiently fundamental to be included among the twelve principal themes of Existentialism.[1] Man is constantly exposed to destruction as a human being because he only continues to exist as such by his own effort, according to their contention. From this state there arises a sensation of anguish, of constant peril and of fatality. It never occurs to the atheistic Existentialist, of course, to consider human existence as under the benign control of divine Providence, and to realize that it may be safe both spiritually and intellectually although physically hazardous. That is the only point of view which is any real safeguard against the prevailing depression of our period; but, once enjoyed, it rises gaily above every sense of fear.

How else can one combat, for instance, the thesis of Heidegger that we are " beings of the void—knowing not from whence we come and irremediably condemned to death. We know ourselves as born of nothing and

[1] *Les Grands Courants de la Pensée Contemporaine*. Grevillot. Quotation from E. Mounier, p. 4.

destined to nothingness?" This may read to the ordinary healthy Christian as complete nonsense, which it certainly is, but it is nevertheless nonsense which is apt to cloud the mind with a kind of melancholy epitome of all the wet afternoons, desolate empty houses, and sighing, leaf-stripped trees, which one has ever met.

When the Existentialist feels nausea at the thought of existence, when he finds all life absurd, from his own point of view he is perhaps right. If everything were without meaning, without definite form, ridiculous; if there existed no values worth living for, and *yet*, as free beings enjoying complete liberty of will, we were bound continually to choose, to decide and to act—surely such a contrast would be sufficient to account for a sense of human despair and tragedy? Take God out of existence, and existence indeed becomes absurd, pointless, repulsive to the verge of nausea.

Yet life has to be lived and, man's whole trend being upwards, his inner consciousness urges him to live it finely and to purpose. Thus it is that the nobler the character and the keener the intellect, the greater the natural powers, the greater also must be the nausea experienced when faced with an existence apparently without ultimate worth or object. It seems indeed difficult to find, within the immediate compass of life, anything which is worth all the striving, the disappointment, the recurring frustrations of Time. Yet the urgency and the finality of death are basic in Existentialist philosophy. Its exponents are fundamentally opposed to what they consider the general tendency to hide from ourselves the primordial truth that life ends, and ends for ever, with this world. Beyond it there is nothing.

An Existentialist, one imagines, might well repudiate this view of his philosophy. He would reply that there are undoubtedly things in life worth living for, even although they are only temporary. The moment of living is worth while in itself. There is a type of Existentialist who is largely a humanist, and almost obsessed with the idea of complete sincerity. He is therefore in many respects tolerant in his scepticism, and will allow others to hold what views they please, provided that they will live their beliefs fully, engage themselves to the utmost, and make the best of things. For what precise reason they should make the best of things, if there is no God and no hereafter, is his secret. His frame of mind appears to consist of a queer mixture of humanism, scepticism and disillusionment.

Speaking quite generally, it may be that one of the reasons why the thought of final extinction, the thought that there is nothing beyond this earth—no God, no eternity—makes man so profoundly unhappy, is just quite simply because it is not true. There is. It is a lie against which his whole nature instinctively revolts, however much he may twist his thoughts, and dragoon his emotions, into a seeming acceptance of it. Perhaps the knowledge of his own immortality can be hidden from a man, but in even the most ignorant there seems to be some obscure sense of God and of a future life. Scepticism is much more a fruit of the intellect than of instinct. It may be therefore that, as we said, one of the reasons why the thought that death ends everything is inclined to send man into despair is simply that it is not true.

How can Time alone satisfy those whose fixed destiny it is to pass beyond it and to live in the Eternal? The instinctive urge of human nature is to seek something outside itself, and above itself, to worship. In primitive peoples this urge may take the form of the worship of some natural object, such as the Sun in the case of the

Parsees, whom one could watch lining the sea's edge in Bombay, and praying as it sank in golden glory below the blue of the far horizon.

As J. Wilhelm remarks: "The original idea of God has taken in the mind of man all the distorted and fanciful forms which a liquid is liable to assume in a collapsible vessel, or clay in the potter's hands. As, in the course of ages, the power of healing has been attributed to almost every substance and combination of substances, so has the divine power been traced in all things. and all things have been worshipped accordingly."

But, at least in this case, they have been worshipped as symbols of the spiritual, and of the divine. Happiness is compatible with such a state, since genuine ignorance is inculpable. But happiness would not seem to be compatible with the unremitting and obstinate worship of self in lieu of God, which is the cult of the deliberate atheist. The first is a reaching out, an effort at transcendence, and an affirmation: the second is a closing in on self, a gesture of materialism, and a denial.

No wonder that among the Existentialists we get the doctrine of the Great Absurd. Father Copleston, S.J., says, regarding the philosophy of Albert Camus: "The human mind has a desperate desire for clarity and for meaning; but the world is opaque; it yields no ground for supposing that it has any purpose. From the confrontation of the human spirit with the world arises the sensation of the Absurd. The world is not absurd in itself; nor is man absurd in himself; but the two taken in conjunction give rise to the absurd. What is absurd is man's deepest longings and hopes and desires, when confronted with the world."[2] The agony of the Existentialist, therefore, is created by himself and carried within himself. He thinks that it has to do with the world in

[2] *Existentialism and Modern Man.* Father Copleston, S.J. p. 16.

which he lives, but in reality it only has to do with his misconception of it.

When it comes to death from the Christian point of view, the story is altogether different. True, most of us have had, at some time or another, one illness or experience among all the rest which was strangely memorable. A time when death, as it were, came close to us; gripped us by the throat; no longer the vague, distant foe on whom we had sometimes meditated—poetically or fearfully according to our temperament. When he comes thus, close and real, so that we feel his breath on our cheek; his strong, icy hands enfolding our own, suddenly grown so weak; he looks at us for a moment as foe, however much we love God, however much we hope to go to Him. That is no more that the natural, physical reaction. Death itself, our real going to God, when at last it comes in earnest, often comes differently: sweetly, without warning of fear, as the friend of our soul. The other was only a foretaste: a moment's piercing of the hard rind of our self-complacency and false sense of security, for which we may thank God.

Dostoyevsky, the Russian, had such an experience—that second of Time when Eternity is only one step beyond—and it coloured his whole outlook for the remainder of his life. As a young man, in St. Petersburg, he had stood before a firing-squad in the Semenovsky Square. None of us has been nearer death than that, without actually dying, but to some of us it may seem that we have once come as near. It is a foretaste which we shall never forget and which God does not mean us to forget. It leaves us humbler, more dependent on Him, less self-assertive to others. We may be grateful for it.

Meanwhile the undeniable fact remains that man is always seeking something beyond himself, something above himself, something everlasting, and that death is the only, and the tenderly happy answer, to those aspirations. He who shall lose his life shall find it—but he must lose it first. Man has a consciousness of eternity; there is in him a perpetual effort to lift himself above the senses and the immediate, to the universal and the everlasting, which no one can deny. The Greeks did their best to mask death, and Plato in particular dreamed of a final victory of spirit over matter; but only Christianity can give a definite form to faith; only Christianity can speak of death, decisively and triumphantly, in terms of gain not loss.

Our Lord, when talking of His own death to His disciples, was completely sure that the coming of the Holy Ghost would repay them a thousand times for His going. He offered them then, as the Catholic Church offers us now, the substitution of spirit for flesh; and He offered it to them as an unequivocal gain. His earthly, bodily presence was to be replaced by the invisible comfort and guidance of the Holy Ghost; He offered them spirit at the cost of flesh, as He offers it to us still. If we have the courage to accept, then from that moment we are recognizing life as eternal; for us the boundaries of matter are in a sense already crossed.

Régis Jolivet, in writing of the essentially spiritual tendencies of man's nature, bases his argument on the teaching of St. Thomas. "The certainty which is the foundation of our hope, and its justification, is that everything, absolutely everything, death as well as life, is included in the sphere of infinite love from which everything proceeds and in which everything is accomplished."[3]

[3] *Le Problème de la Mort.* Régis Jolivet. p. 46 and pp. 109-110.

CHAPTER X

THE SEA AND A BUCKET

I<small>T</small> was a lovely spring day; the sky was trying to pretend that it was Italian, while the flowering cherries near the pond were trying to remind one of the Rhine. Bygone days! The postulant's profile, as she sat on the stone parapet of the steps leading down to the lawn, suggested that bygone days were not perhaps the safest thing to think about for those still young in Religion. Somehow I felt sure that she *was* thinking of them and that it was the Italian-looking sky which was responsible.

I had interrupted a conversation between her and Sister Imelda, and had said, "Go on", when they looked round in welcome.

"We have a very pretty garden," remarked Sister Imelda pensively, evidently pursuing a not altogether successful topic, "the sea, however much you long for it, is only water after all, and the sky and the sun are the same wherever you go."

"And, of course, if I would like I could always get permission to go and sit beside a bucket in the laundry."

"A bucket in the laundry?" Sister Imelda looked mystified.

"Water," said the postulant briefly, "that's all the sea is."

"You might also get permission for a little salt from the kitchen," I put in pleasantly, but she did not smile.

Sister Imelda glanced at me. When it is a matter of

the flesh and the devil she is on sure ground; they do not change; but when it comes to the world, I have noticed a growing tendency on her part to escape and leave it to me. It appears a doubtful sort of compliment, but when I taxed her with it she said that it was only on account of my greater youth. As I did not know whether that were intended as a compliment either, I said no more. Indeed, her world, full of hansom cabs, and hunt-breakfasts, sunny lawns and candles to light you to bed, and with the general leisureliness of days upon the hours of which no restless wireless or television, no sound of bumping motor-lorry or whirring plane had ever intruded, is not quite the world which our postulants have so recently left.

"I'll go and feed the chickens," she said, and got up. We watched her down the path.

I looked at Sister Elizabeth and I felt infinitely sorry for her. I had not in the least forgotten—not in the very least; but I did know that there is not much that anyone else can do about it. It is one of those completely personal and solitary moments in life. Pious platitudes are of no good at all, and may even act as irritants, nor the Will of God in capitals, nor being reminded of the joys of heaven. But, after all, I reflected, she and I had been quite good friends in the days when we saw each other only in the parlour: I decided to take the plunge.

"What's the matter, Libby?" said I, addressing the pebbles at my feet. She groaned. I waited a minute. "Bad day?"

"Ugh."

"Anything special?"

"Um, Ugh."

"Quite," I agreed. We sat in silence. "Is it the Habit?"

"Ugh."

"Quite," I said again. I am afraid that I have not a very original mind. Sister Imelda would have hit the nail on the head at once, of course, with some happy phrase or a quotation from Daniel.

"Well, cheer up, you needn't," I remarked at last.

"Needn't what?"

"Take it."

"That's just it. I don't know *which* I want."

"Doesn't matter which you want: it is which God wants. But you are the only person He is likely to tell. Nobody else can decide it for you."

"That's just it," groaned the poor postulant.

"Now look here, Libby, pull yourself together. It is no good getting in a state about it. I'll open that enclosure door this minute if you really want to go."

"But I don't."

"Well, it's quite simple then. Take the Habit."

"Ugh."

"Well, you can't do neither," I said practically. She dropped her head between her hands. "Look here, my dear, this is purely a matter between God and yourself, but could I make a few general remarks on vocations if that would assist?" She lifted her head enough to nod. Anthony appeared from the shrubbery and sat himself in friendly fashion between the two of us.

"To begin with, among a great many different motives for coming into religion, most of them beside the point, there are two which can be roughly distinguished almost from the beginning. They separate the getters from the givers, if you understand what I mean. We are all of us either one or the other in life anyway, wherever we live. Now, when it is a case of being in Religion, the givers have a worse time at first because, when it actually comes to giving, as a fact and not merely on paper or in imagination, it turns out to be so very much more, and so very much worse, than anything we had ever intended to give. We had said 'everything', and we had meant everything, but we had no idea that everything could possibly include so much." Sister Elizabeth groaned again.

"Oh, yes." They were the first words she had spoken which were an assent, and at least, I consoled myself, it was a shade better than a simple *ugh*.

"It is quite truly a case of the whole sea against a bucket of water in the laundry, and that for ever: for ever on earth at least." She shivered. "No, *don't* shiver. That's just it. Face it; and if you are going to choose the bucket of water, *choose* it. If you once allow yourself to shiver at the thought, you will shiver for the rest of your life. And there you are—a *religieuse manquée*."

"I don't want to be that," said Elizabeth glumly. In deep and silent sympathy we stroked opposite ends of the cat.

"The getters have their worst time very much later, and it is altogether a more serious affair. It is so serious, in fact, that the only cases of real disaster which I personally have met, have almost certainly been due to it. You see, there comes the awful moment when they realize, at least some of them do, that they are not going to get it after all—*never* going to get it."

"Get what?"

"Whatever they unconsciously came in for. We don't *get* in religion; we *give*. It is the spiritual alone which we receive, and half the time we cannot even feel ourselves receiving it."

"What sort of things do you suppose they think they are going to get?"

"I can't tell you. Probably it is all only semi-conscious of course. Perhaps it is a sensation of sanctity which they hope to enjoy; perhaps a quiet life without, as they imagine, bustle or hurry; perhaps they have an imaginary devotion to the recitation of the Divine Office—I don't know. But mostly, I should guess, a kind of unconscious spiritual ambition of some sort or another."

"Oh, dear! " said the postulant, looking forlorn.

"Don't worry. You are a giver if you are anything at all. The only question for you is just whether you *can* give it or not."

"I suppose that's it," said Elizabeth. "But how," she wailed suddenly, "am I ever to know—until it is too late, one way or the other? "

"Libby," I said severely, "do not begin the too late business. That is sheer morbidity. Nothing is ever too late until we are dead. In any case, you have plenty of time in which to make the decision, and you are on the right side of it still."

"This is not a question of time, it is a question of eternity; I have sense enough to know that." She stroked Anthony's ears and he rubbed himself against her, conscious of something wrong.

"There is another thing to remember, and that is that we all have our bad moments for making decisions, or indeed for thinking of anything sensibly. They pass after a little. Are you hungry? " I demanded suddenly.

"Oh, no."

"You can't be cold, and not likely to be dead-tired at this time of day. No, it is just that appalling Italian sky; I am sure it is."

"Oh, yes! " There was positive relief in her voice. "Spring, you know. Tell me," she added confidentially, "what would *you* do if you could do exactly as you liked for a whole day? "

"Exactly what I am going to do."

She stared. "Not really? "

"Really."

"But why? "

"Because, you see, this *is* my life: God's life for me: my life for Him and so my life for myself. The choice you are faced with now is a thing of the past for me, isn't it? I don't need to make it again."

She returned to stroking Anthony's ears and this time he began to purr. I listened with relief. Cats, so temperamental themselves, never make a temperamental mistake about others.

"How does one get there?" Her tone was business-like.

"Just by doing it—living it—nothing else. There is no short cut. But one has to make up one's mind, once and for all, that that is how it is going to be. The rest comes with God's grace. Even then, as I was going to say before, there are corners to be got round for a long time. That applies to life anywhere. Special times of the day or night are bad for some people; for others it may be a particular physical sensation, such as hunger, fatigue, cold, anything you like—or don't like. The only remedy I know of is to get hold of a practical awareness of the fact; pin it down; and then discount it altogether. At such times, just shut off thinking. One might as well, in any case, because such thinking never gets one anywhere."

"You talk as if thinking were just a tap that could be turned on and off."

"So it is—at least it may be. *Emotion* is not, I grant you. It is much harder to turn off the emotion tap. But anyone can say: 'I am not going to think about that while I feel like this, because I know that if I do I shall only think nonsense. When I stop feeling like this, I shall see things quite differently.' And when we stop feeling like that, we *do* see things quite differently, and are usually relieved to have been saved from making fools of ourselves in one way or another. That applies equally anywhere—here or in the world. It is merely commonsense."

Sister Elizabeth stood up and shook herself: literally shook herself: then she sat down again—this time on Anthony's tail. He only gave the mildest of miaows, because he likes Sister Elizabeth exceedingly, next best to Sister Imelda in fact, and he is no fool. He looked at her with melting black eyes.

"Sorry, old man," she said. "Tell me then, exactly how can I settle this once and for all?"

"You can't—not once and for *all*. You are not a heavenly spirit. Your will goes on being free, and you will have to go on using it until you die, my dear, in one direction or another. But what you can settle, once and for all, is the *principle* of the decision. Afterwards, you will have to sustain it by day to day action, by day to day struggle if you like, but the fundamental decision will be off your mind. You will know what you ought to do, and what you hope to do, in spite of the fact that the world, the flesh, and the devil, will spend their whole time trying to tug you off it."

"Um." The um was calm, however, I noted with relief. So did Anthony. He purred softly in the sunshine.

"Well, how does one get the principle settled anyway?"

"Think. Stand back and look at it: look at it all round. And remember, there are two parts to every decision. There is what one really wants with one's soul and one's mind, that is with one's whole inner self; and in addition there is all the exterior fuss and bother of getting it, the toil and the sweat and tears, as Winston called it, and the pain of pursuit. It does not matter what it is, or where we are, that is true of life. Love, ambition, money, whatever it is we are trying to find and to possess, we have to work, to suffer and to concentrate. But when *God* is our aim and our end . . ."

"Um."

"Decide what it is that God wants; that means, for anyone who loves Him, decide what it is that *you* want with the best part of yourself, for that is the desire which He will have put into you. When you have got that clear, decide whether it is worth all the rest. But do not forget, my dear, that what I call all the rest is only intermittent. Do not take too gloomy, too impressive a view of your vocation. Give your sense of humour a chance as well. There is plenty of joy in this life and God does not, as if He were a miser, save up the whole of His treasure only for the end."

"Sister Imelda for instance?" Anthony cocked his head at the name.

"Sister Imelda," I agreed. "Before you try to settle this, get the *general* enclosed vocation clear in your mind; the vocation itself, not yours in particular. There are contemplatives everywhere, in the world, in the desert, isolated examples. But this is the Church's own recognized form of the contemplative life, the public form of it, as it were, lived for the Church, lived for the world. Libby—you remember that priest you met on your way to Rome? I have found out who he is—do you want to know?" She looked interested at last, so I told her. "He said two Masses for you, not one, and he begs you to go on praying for him."

"You mean you know him?"

"I have known him almost all my life."

"Then he doesn't need *my* prayers," said Elizabeth smiling. I shook my head.

"That is a thoroughly silly remark. Don't get into the way of saying silly, superficial things, however obvious, just because they are easy to say. Think it out. You know that there is no such thing really as ' your prayer ', ' my prayer ', in the sense you suggest. There is prayer, Libby, and we all of us need all of it that we can get."

"Sorry," said Sister Elizabeth.

"When I write, what shall I tell him? " I asked, eyeing her firmly; "that you are still going to pray for him? "

"Oh, yes,—but of course! "

I absent-mindedly pulled Anthony's tail hard because I wanted to say something that was not very easy to say. "Miaow," said Anthony, and fell asleep again immediately. Nerves are not his weak point, I must admit.

"Suppose," said I at last, "that on that train journey you had just been one of the other passengers—sight-seeing, or going home again, or something—do you think Monsignor would have asked your prayers? "

"Oh, no." There is this to be said for Sister Elizabeth; she has no delusions about her own importance.

"Well, have you thought out why? "

"I suppose. . . ."

"You stick. When people stick it usually means that they can only think of something foolish which they are too sensible to express. I will tell you why: not because he thought you looked exceptionally holy, or un-usually pious for one so young, or that God loved you in some special and select manner." She winced slightly. "Don't wince, because I am going to give you the per-fectly simple and straightforward reason which you could repeat to all the world without one blush."

She made a quick movement, and Anthony uttered a final, prolonged howl. Any more conversation over his head, with one person violently pulling his tail and the other constantly tweaking his ears, was really more than any cat could stand, and he said so. We both apologized and began to stroke him the right way up to make amends. He shut his eyes again and emitted a forgiving purr. Anthony is a Carmelite after all, and so he never bears malice.

"It was because you were to become a specialist, that is all. We ask a singer to sing for us, and a poet to give us verse, and a mathematician to work out our sums, and a government to govern. And we ask a contemplative nun to pray for us for the simple reason that that is what she is there for. If you had been just a nice young girl on a trip to Rome, he might have offered in a fatherly way to conduct you round the Vatican, though, knowing him, I seriously doubt it; but I am quite sure that he would not have offered you a Mass for your intention."

"Um."

"You *do* want this vocation, I can tell you that; but the trouble is that of course you want a lot of other things as well. So do all the other specialists, and they get them. Whoever heard of a poet, or a painter, or a mathematician, or a scientist, who was only that and nothing else? He has all his natural, ordinary life as well if he wants it, and does a dozen other things in between his specializing. But we can't. We have to do just this and nothing else. *Sponsa Christi* has, if possible, made us more of specialists than ever. Not only has it quite definitely confirmed what it calls the apostolate of the vocation, but it has classified still further even the contemplative communities themselves. There are those who lead the purely contemplative life, and those who add to it some exterior and active form of work. You won't be able to manage the purely contemplative life unless you are called to it, I can tell you that. You might as well think that you must be able to sing yourself because you admire Wagner, or to write a play because you love to read Shakespeare."

"Oh, I believe I'm *called* all right," said Sister Elizabeth a trifle sulkily, "it's whether I *can*—ugh——"

"Once you have seen that, and acknowledged it, half the battle is won. Your half, that is. The other, God will win for you all in His good time. The people who go, Libby, are the people who begin pretending that they are not sure if they are called. They don't mean to pretend, of course, but the devil does a little persuading as well."

"I suppose sometimes people get inside by mistake, who really and honestly aren't called?"

"They do. Rarely. But you have just said that you are. And if, when you are alone, the devil tries to persuade you that you can do this particular vocation just as well in the world, please explain to him that, if one cannot become a regular soldier, one may possibly become a territorial, and do very well at it, and be extremely useful to one's country; but that if, on the contrary, one has decided to make the army one's profession, one does not precisely leave Sandhurst in order to become a better soldier in the territorials."

Her wistful question as to what I should do if I had a whole free day to myself, however, had touched a spring in my mind. Why not, after all?

"It is of no use to suggest your going back to the world to decide this: the world has just as strong an atmosphere as we have, and what *you* want is no atmosphere at all for a couple of days while you think. You need to draw right back, to be between the two attractions, before you can judge sanely. Take two clear days to get it straight. Say to yourself that, if you wish, at the end of them you can walk out of that door as free as air. Don't come to the choir, or to work, or to recreation, or to anything except Mass and meals, and in between do just as you please. Sit in the garden—read—I'll give you some pleasant books—pray in the Oratory—paint if it amuses you—talk to the chickens; take Anthony for a walk, he favours the rubbish-heap, and you can sit among the ashes if you like and pretend that you are Job. Quote him: you will feel better. 'Old tales and cold comfort, you are all alike. Words are but wind; there is no end to them and they cost thee nothing'." The postulant showed unmistakable signs of reviving life. "Let me see no more of you until to-morrow evening—unless, of course, you get bored all by yourself."

"Get bored by myself!" she waved her arms. "Good-bye. Thank you. Come on, Anthony."

I watched her down the bank: we usually keep to the paths, but even as my mind noted it I knew that it did not matter. I must admit that Sister Elizabeth frequently brings before me all the things which we do not usually do: but I have at least learnt this much from life: if we will not accept what a person is not, we sometimes spoil all that they are, and could be. I went and found Sister Imelda.

"Sister Elizabeth is going to have two days' rest," I said in a matter of fact voice, "no particular work, no choir except Mass, no recreation. Just leave her free, will you?"

Sister Imelda put down her watering-can and slowly and deliberately stared at me. "No work, no choir, no meals, no recreation. Is she ill?"

"Not in the least."

"Is she ill in her soul then?"

"Certainly not."

"Is it something in those books?" There was deep suspicion in her tone.

"Just leave her alone, Sister," I begged, "she will be all right. And I didn't say she wasn't coming to the refectory." She eyed me narrowly, then picked up her watering-can and moved away. After a few steps however she turned back.

"If I ask the provisor, may I have the key of the provisory, please, for a minute?"

"The provisory key? Whatever for?"

"Just something I want out of it. Can I take it if it is there?"

"Oh, certainly," I said hastily, my mind still on Sister Elizabeth, "anything you like."

It must have been half an hour later that I met her toiling up the stairs towards the Novitiate. There was a most unusual bulge beneath her scapular and, wondering, I drew her into an empty cell.

"You should not tire yourself up all these stairs," I said reproachfully, "and what on earth have you got there?"

"It doesn't tire me, truly it doesn't," she assured me eagerly, "and it's nothing at all; you said I could have it."

I put my hand beneath her scapular and pulled out a paper bag. The top was tied round with blue ribbon, and attached to it was a small printed label. I opened the top and peeped. Inside there was an apple, an orange, three or four home-made biscuits, a small packet of chocolate which I recognized as part of a present to Sister Imelda at Christmas, a holy picture of Baby Jesus, and three very ancient and sticky peppermints. I shut the bag again and retied the ribbon in silence. Sister Imelda watched me anxiously. Then I read the label: "For the picnic, with my love." I handed it back to her and opened the door. "I promise I won't speak," she said earnestly, and went down the corridor towards the cells.

For two days I was haunted by an elusive black figure which hid behind bushes in the garden and disappeared mysteriously whenever I approached; which slipped in and out of the oratory where I was trying to pray, and fell over me in dark corners of the passages where I did not expect to meet anyone; which peered at me from the door of the loft, and at one moment seemed almost to be contemplating a paddle in the pond.

On the evening of the second day, just as I was finishing a page of very dull accounts, there was a knock at the door. I replied with the customary *Deo Gratias*, and Sister Elizabeth stood before me. Upon her face there was what I can only describe as a pleased grin and she was accompanied by Anthony the Cat who knows perfectly well that he is not allowed in this room.

"Thank you for the books," she said, and put them down upon the desk, "and I have chosen the bucket." So that was that. It was not perhaps the traditional way of expressing it, but she meant it, and that, after all, is the main thing. We have to take people as they are, in life, and not as they might be. In any case, I reflected happily, Sister Elizabeth and all her modern counterparts might very easily be something worse.

CHAPTER XI

THE SOLITARY EXISTENTIALIST

EXISTENTIALISM is a definite sign of the times. All the people who write about it, speak about it, believe in it, or still more ardently disbelieve in it, seem to be agreed as to that. Even those who deplore it the most, admit that it is congenial to the general trend of contemporary thought.

The modern man, Père Grevillot suggests, recognizes himself to a great extent in the picture drawn of human nature by the Existentialists, hence their attraction for him. "We no longer live in a world proud of its science and its results, nor in a gay world entirely given up to the joy of life; amusement is for him (the man of to-day) distraction in the Pascalian sense of the word; he amuses himself in order to escape from the anguish which stifles him."[1]

Father Copleston, S.J., also remarks: "The popularity of Existentialism in France can certainly be connected with the political events of 1940 and succeeding years, just as the interest aroused in Germany by the thought of Heidegger can be connected with the political and social situation in Germany after the first world war."[2]

The fact is that Existentialism begins and breeds best in despair, just as Marxism breeds in discontent. Or perhaps one should say that the first affects most the mind of the thinker, while the second is designed to sway the

[1] *Les Grands Courants de la Pensée Contemporaine.* Grevillot. p. 56.
[2] *Existentialism and Modern Man.* F. C. Copleston, S.J. p. 17.

mind of the mass. They mutually despise each other, yet their origins are much the same.

The point, however, is that we, following belatedly the example of the rest of Europe, are now perhaps in danger of drifting towards the general state of mind in which such a philosophy as Existentialism might take hold of the imaginations of our young pagans, as the writings of Bernard Shaw once took hold of them a generation ago. It has a certain descriptive charm and an atmosphere of its own.

There is a story of Stalin during his Siberian imprisonment. He wrote to his friends, the Alliluyevas, asking them to send him picture postcards. He wanted nothing else. On the Yenissey, where he was, there was nothing for the eye to meet but the frozen emptiness of the tundra. "In this accursed country," he admitted, "I have been overcome by a silly longing to see some landscape, be it only on paper." So, after all, our Stalins have their emotions. And, to the rising generation, things on paper seem to have as much value as real things. Certainly at times the freedom of thought seems more dear to them than the essence of it; and there is a great freedom of thought among Existentialists.

In the rather dreary state of the world there is a certain allure about the picture-postcard representation of life. Stalin's postcard was not in itself a landscape, nor did it even specifically seek to assert that landscapes are real and actually exist. It merely showed a picture, in the delightful modern way, and allowed him to imagine a landscape by means of it. "This," says our representation, "looks very much like a landscape, don't you think? —and from it it would appear that landscapes do in fact exist. You can colour it, and put the atmosphere to it, and deduce what you like from it, of course, to suit yourselves. The great thing is that your conclusions should

H

be entirely subjective. What does this landscape convey to *you*? That is all that matters."

There are two points about Existentialism which undoubtedly have charm, even to the superficial. The first is the matter, which so vividly concerns life itself; the second is the manner which, although it is as old as Plato, who frequently used the dramatic and narrative style, yet is still a change when applied to the normally dry subject of philosophy.

According to Existentialism the principal problem for us all is that of our concrete existence. "How do I exist? Why do I exist?" As every philosophy deals to a certain extent with these problems, every philosophy can be called in a sense Existentialist, but the actual name has been reserved for those whose thought is, in the terms of E. Mounier, "a reaction of the philosophy of Man against an excess of the philosophy of ideas". M. Camus is even more explicit: "To judge whether life is, or is not, worth living, is to reply to the fundamental question of philosophy".[3]

E. Mounier then gives us a long list of the principal conclusions reached by Existentialism, among which is the insufficiency of reason alone to explain existence. In this, of course, Existentialists are completely right, only it never occurs to them to turn to God to explain it further. Instead they decide that man must regulate his conduct according to his own "most profound spiritual consciousness". He must, in other words, just guess at life, following his heart and not his head.

Man's sense of isolation is another problem which leads him to consider his relation to those around him. Every human creature tends to feel himself as being solitary and impenetrable to others, although he knows that in reality he is not alone. Again, it never occurs to the

[3] *Les Grands Courants de la Pensée Contemporaine.* Grevillot. p. 3.

atheist to reflect that this sense of isolation is caused for him by the absence of God. He *is*, in fact, isolated. He has missed the whole point of life; he sees a distorted world surrounding him, without rhyme or reason; he is like a distracted child in a nightmare fairy-tale, caught in the shadows and pursued by ghosts. He asks himself frantically what it is all about, and comes to the conclusion that it is all about himself. He then concentrates on himself and calls it the philosophy of existence.

Nevertheless he cannot altogether escape the presence of those others; he knows, as he admits, that in reality he is not alone. "The human being," declared Heidegger, "is a being-with" (*mitsein*). Added to which, he concludes that he has actual need of others in order to explain himself to himself. He sees himself best, as it were, reflected in them, and by watching and judging them comes to understand his own reactions. Others, he finds, are "the mediators between him and himself". Thus he can only attain to the knowledge of himself "by the judgment of another, by the hatred of another".

Here again, it never occurs to these sorry logicians that one attains best to a knowledge of self by the love of God and the grace of God who made us all. The hatred felt for us by another does not really decipher us to ourselves in the least—although it may possibly to a certain extent help us to decipher him. And the first and principal thing it will tell us about him is that he needs our prayers, since hatred is very far from God. "By their fruits ye shall know them", and, let us make no mistake: as surely as Christianity leads to love, so surely does atheistic Existentialism or Marxism ultimately lead to hate.

The atheist Existentialists assert that their philosophy is a form of Humanism and not a philosophy of Pessimism. An atheist philosophy is always, from the Christian point of view, a philosophy of pessimism and can be nothing else; but it is maintained by its followers that Existentialism is, at all events, no more so than any other pagan creed. It is also claimed, and this has its own attraction no doubt, that it cannot be considered as a quietist philosophy since it defines man continually in terms of action; nor as a despairing description of man, since it contains the optimistic doctrine that man's destiny is to be found in himself, and lies in his own hands; nor as an attempt to discourage man from acting boldly since, on the contrary, it teaches that his only hope is to be found in doing so; that the only thing, in fact, which permits a man to live at all is action. Certainly it must be conceded quite honestly that no one could accuse Existentialism of not being virile, and therein may lie a certain potential attraction to a virile generation.

Nevertheless, and in spite of these protestations, the idea of the *néant*—the void, nothingness—recurs unceasingly, and produces the effect of a profoundly disillusioned outlook. For the atheist philosopher, death remains a final and irrevocable extinction. This would seem to preclude any absolute achievement for man except the sorry achievement of complete destruction. But meanwhile, according to Heidegger, there are many forms of minor completeness still open to us. In this connection, Régis Jolivet makes the rather fascinating suggestion that the idea of incompleteness lies with *us*, and not with things in themselves.[4] For instance, a crescent moon is, in itself, a finished and perfect thing. It is only I who, leaping forward in mind to the full moon, make of it something unfinished. The incompleteness is in my mind and not in the baby moon.

One can, however, go on conjecturing in this way for ever, and at the end of it all we have got no further, and

[4] *Le Problème de la Mort.* Régis Jolivet. p. 24.

THE SOLITARY EXISTENTIALIST 117

we still die. We are like the celebrity who lived in the Cromwell Road and invited a friend to dinner. On being asked to give directions as to how to get to him, he replied simply: "You walk down the Cromwell Road, and you go on walking until you drop dead: there is my house."

With regard to the anguish written of so frequently by all Existentialists, Roger Troisfontaines offers this interesting explanation of it which he believes fits at least some cases. It may be remembered that we spoke earlier of his classification of men in general. One of the categories he included was that of the emotional-inactives who do not produce, but *feel*, events. He believes that possibly much of their disgust with life has its origin in the fact of their being thus inactive by nature.[5] They are swollen with desires and ambitions, in imagination, which they are unable to realize in fact, and so they come to regard themselves as isolated, alone—even abandoned by the rest of the world. For the man who thinks along these lines, life tends to become a farce: the Great Absurd: a comedy at which he can only shrug his shoulders contemptuously. But for the man who *feels* in such a way, it appears as a tragedy, and a tragedy without hope. In either case the point of agreement between the two views is to be found in their subjectivity. "Truth," proclaimed Kierkegaard, "is subjectivity."

Troisfontaines summarizes the point of view of the Existentialist thus:[6] the sphere which interests us the most escapes all conceptional definition, all constructive effort, all systemization. The most profound reality of all can neither be deduced, nor contemplated, nor dreamed. It can never be object: it is impossible, therefore, to imagine a philosophy of it which is, in the strict

[5] *Existentialisme et Pensée Chrétienne.* Troisfontaines. p. 16.
[6] *Ibid.* p. 19.

sense of the world, communicable. In order to attain to it, I myself must live it—I alone. I must apprehend it personally in an original experience lived by me.

"Speaking generally," he writes, "any doctrine which seeks to integrate the various aspects of reality in an experience *which has been lived*, can call itself existential."[7]   Or again, in a final definition, "Existentialism is a passionate return by the individual to his liberty in an attempt to discover, from the unfolding of his own conduct, the meaning of his existence."[8]

The Existentialist is, therefore, always an individualist. Personal liberty is his fetish, and in liberty he recognizes the origin of all values. His only criterion of reality and truth is his own personal experience. Truth thus becomes completely subjective: it is to be found only in an absolute fidelity to oneself. The implications, to the ordinary individual, appear quite appalling. Fidelity to God, of course, does not come into it at all: fidelity to others can only be relative: in fact, it amounts to this: I am my own God.

This new philosophy is, as we said before, interested above all in the meaning of existence, but it claims that such a meaning can only be found in and through the individual. Troisfontaines suggests that many of its statements about the *absurd* and the *néant* which have scandalized its opponents are no more than a clearing of the way for the establishment of wholly subjective values, by first showing the inanity of objective declarations.[9] Personal experience alone can form the basis of truth. Just as the dream of happiness does not confer happiness, so the purely intellectual representation of truth will not give us truth itself.

[7] *Existentialisme et Pensée Chrétienne*.   Troisfontaine.   p. 31.
[8] *Ibid*.   p. 44.
[9] *Ibid*.   pp. 46-47.

It is, of course, obvious that St. Augustine, and much later Newman, had something of this point of view when they spoke of a "return to the heart", of "realization". This inter-relation between theory and practice has, indeed, been quite genuinely lived by most great philosophers. But Existentialism is more explicitly conscious of it than any other philosophy, and confers upon it, as upon the actions of our individual existence, an exclusively ontological value.

Apart from the interest of many of the theories advanced by the Existentialists, the very personal style adopted by one or two of its most prominent exponents has an undoubted attraction when taken in conjunction with a subject such as philosophy. The manner, already in vogue in America, is what one might call the synchronized style. That is to say, the simultaneous and no longer successive description of events happening, in reality, at widely separated points of the earth. The real interest of this lies not so much in its connection with contemporary literature as in its connection with contemporary life. It shows the influence, even upon the arts, of aviation and the radio. It shows the tendency, in spite of Iron Curtains and ideological divisions, to reach out towards a certain strange world-unity, a consciousness of the solidarity of human interests. Everything tends to become global—including ourselves.

Whether this is entirely a good thing is another matter. One is conscious of a slight feeling that it could perhaps go too far. The man who is never at home ends by having no home worth the name, and it is, after all, the singular prerogative of God to be everywhere at once.

CHAPTER XII

THE SOLITARY IN THE CLOISTER

SISTER Imelda was engaged in telling us how to
shorten the memory: how to forget. It is not a thing
which one usually has need to learn, but the postulant seemed to think that there were moments when the
knowledge might be useful to her. Sister Imelda was
feeding her chickens with tit-bits while she talked, among
which were the remains of a rissole made with cheese.
Sister Elizabeth, who is growing quite knowledgeable
about the fowls eyed them disapprovingly.

"If you give them any more of that," she remarked at
last, "it's not buttered eggs they will lay us but Welsh-
rabbits." Sister Imelda continued unmoved with her
distribution. The book says that we must at first allow
for the full play of individuality in our aspirants: so
we do our best to live up to it. So do the aspirants. We
trust that our new methods are bearing fruit, but we
shall of course have to wait some years in order to be
sure. Meanwhile the number of times we are obliged to
shut our eyes, or to turn them away quickly, or to over-
look, is having an undoubted effect on our vision.

Sister Imelda had explained that when she wants to
shorten her memory and start afresh, so to speak, she just
shuts her mind to the past for a few days.

"But how?"

"Just shut it."

"But *how?*"

Sister Imelda threw down the last of her scraps and

stared. "Now don't tell me that among all the marvellous things they have managed to teach you about your
psyche and your personality and your individuality and
your ego, they have not managed to teach you how to
close your own mind for a short time when you want
to?"

For once the postulant looked almost abashed. "I
don't seem to remember. . . ." she stammered.

"By the use of your will, of course," said Sister Imelda,
"and I suppose you will be asking me next how to use
your will?"

"Well how *do* you?" said the postulant.

"You use your free will in exactly the same way that
you use the free-wheel of a bicycle," explained Sister
Imelda, becoming exceedingly scientific. "Yes, I did
bicycle," she continued a little coldly, catching sight of
Sister Elizabeth's face, "and I did have a free-wheel, so
you need not imagine that I rode one of those affairs with
only one enormous wheel in the middle and a tiny one
behind, and no rubber tyres, which you could only get
on to by clinging to a lamp-post. Not at all. Now when
one was free-wheeling, one did not need to be told that
one's wheel was free because one could feel that it was,
and it is exactly the same principle when it comes to our
own will. We don't need to be told that it is free because we can feel that it is. So going downhill—downhill," she repeated, eyeing the postulant severely, "no
doubt you allowed it to run as it liked, as we so often do
the will, although you held it also in check, I trust, with
the brakes?—if you had any sense you did."

"Oh, yes," agreed Sister Elizabeth warmly.

"Well, then, when you wanted to control the wheel
once more, what did you do? You engaged the clutch
and set the pedals in motion by pedalling hard *yourself*,
and so regained the ascendant."

"I see," said the postulant a little doubtfully. Perhaps her bicycle was different.

"Well, if you don't see," concluded Sister Imelda cheerfully, "it is not my fault. I've explained."

"You were telling us about the memory," I suggested hastily. "You know, the thing you think with." On second thoughts, I was not quite sure whether one thinks with the memory or remembers with the think, but I trusted the postulant would not know either. Apparently she did not.

"How to shorten the memory when there is something which it is better not to remember? Oh, that is quite simple. If one has a grievance, for instance, or if one fancies an injury, the thought of it will sometimes tease and tease, until one has the sense just to shut it off quite firmly. Then one is left in peace."

I saw the inevitable *How* beginning to form on the postulant's lips and cut in quickly. "I shall call you 'Whitwey?' if you aren't careful. A man once told me a story of his childhood, and he told the story quite clearly up to a certain point, but there it completely broke down. He just could not remember at all how the incident had ended. He said he had often tried to recapture the memory but had never succeeded. I made a remark about it one day to a student of psychology, who assured me that the explanation was probably simple enough. Something unpleasant had happened at that point; the child had unconsciously but repeatedly put it out of his mind, to such an extent indeed that now the grown man quite genuinely could not remember what had happened."

"That is it. You close the door on thought," agreed Sister Imelda briskly; "it is perfectly easy. Every time it comes into your head you say *No* and turn away and think of something else. Then you have to begin your memory afresh, of course, because you could not go on shutting the door of your mind for ever. At first the point where you close down is a very short distance from the present moment, and so without meaning it you keep on trying to get back behind it. But as the days pass, and fresh things happen, and your mind becomes quite full again, the new pleasant memory grows longer and longer, so that soon there is no need at all for the closed, locked barrier at the end of it. You can open it wide again to all your past: the bit you wanted to forget will just not be there—unless, of course, you go deliberately raking it up."

"It sounds all right," said the postulant judicially, but before she could add more, the Turn-Sister approached. She murmured a few discreet words in my ear, handed me the parlour key, and as discreetly removed herself.

"Sister Elizabeth," said I, "prepare yourself for the worst. It is your dear mother."

"Help! " cried Sister Elizabeth briefly as she rose to her feet. "That will be the answer to my letter, telling her. . . . I never thought she would *come* . . . all that way too! "

"An excellent thing," I assured her blandly; "much easier to talk than to write. She wants to see us both, but separately. Now which is to go first? "

"Tonic before meals, sedative after," advised Sister Imelda, suddenly joining in the conversation.

"Which is it to be? " I repeated, ignoring a remark which appeared beside the point. There was a pause.

"I shouldn't exactly call you a sedative," observed the postulant, regarding me thoughtfully. I felt obliged to ignore that too, since in religion we do not make personal remarks. As I have often observed to myself before, the number of things which one finds that we do not do in religion, is astounding when somebody else insists on doing them all.   I got up.

"I shall go first," I announced firmly and as if I had made the decision entirely unaided, "and Sister Elizabeth will come in when she is called.   Please pray I shall say the right thing."

"I expect she'll do most of the saying," prophesied the postulant gloomily.

"Holy Ghost! " promised Sister Imelda, clasping her small hands together and smiling encouragingly.

Arrived at the parlour, I hesitated as to whether to open the grille or not; there are occasions when the rule can legitimately be relaxed; a melancholy voice from the other side settled the point.

"You are going to open that dreadful thing, aren't you? " it said.   I laughed and swung it back.   "Can't I see your face? "

"I am really sorry but I am afraid not."

"I can't talk to a dreadful drapery."   The voice ceased and a dismal silence ensued.

"Oh, yes, you can," I replied comfortingly.   "When the grille is shut it is rather like a telephone call I admit; but when it is open it is almost as good as a confessional, don't you think?   So nice, and cosy, and private."

"I have never found confessionals cosy," said the flat voice.   "Will Elizabeth have a dreadful thing over her face too? "

I reassured her and at last she settled down and began to talk in earnest.   Her point of view, understandable enough, slowly emerged.   Indeed, as her daughter had foreseen, she did most of the saying, and did it very well. Her grievance, of course, was that Elizabeth was going to be wasted: her talents, her personality, all that she might have done for others in a normal, sensible life in the world.   For her own part, she said firmly, she could

not even see that a specifically Catholic sort of action
was necessary to make one a useful member of society;
surely any cultured, high-principled influence, without
exaggeration, did its part in helping to keep civilization
in being?

"It does; but when there is so much exaggeration
everywhere, in Communism for instance, or sheer paganism, isn't a little exaggeration in another direction perhaps necessary to counteract. . . ?" But she swept on
without a pause.

If something specifically Catholic were required, surely
there were forms of activity more useful to the world
than this? What were we doing in any case? What
contribution did we claim to be making to the world's
welfare? She peered behind me at the bare, white-
washed wall, and the crucifix which hung, lonely, upon
it. Surely there were plenty of forms of Catholic Action
which Elizabeth could undertake if she felt that she must
do something definitely religious? But to sit all day long
in the dark doing nothing. . . ."

"We don't sit in the dark, really we don't. . . ."

"Your choir was perfectly dark for Mass, I was there
this morning and I saw it; and you are in the dark now,
with a veil over your face, doing nothing."

"I am listening to you," I interrupted earnestly, "and
I don't consider that doing nothing, not by any means.
As to your daughter, I quite agree that she could go and
be a factory-worker in disguise, I mean an apostle disguised as a factory-worker, but, after all, doesn't that
seem to you just as exaggerated in its own way?"

"I never proposed that Elizabeth should be a disguised
apostle," replied her mother coldly, "you think in such
extremes. All I want is for her to be quite ordinary
and everyday; nothing more." There was a pause.

"Then you should have given her an ordinary, everyday mother," I suggested mildly. The voice had ceased. The visitor leaned slowly towards the grille.

"Do you know, I never thought of that," she said in quite a friendly tone. Then the grievance reasserted itself.

We went on talking: the talkers running side by side like two trains on parallel tracks. I had the melancholy conviction that if we ran side by side like this for ever, those two tracks would never converge. No points existed on our mutual railway-system which could switch us on to each other's line. We were no longer even trying to convince: we were merely stating and re-stating unalterable views. I almost ceased to state mine, and listened.

Christ came down from heaven to save all humanity; it was the earth He was interested in. In such days as these even quite good Catholics were trying to escape from the very world for which He had given His life. Religious people herded together; they stuck like glue in their churches, their convents, their trains to Lourdes and to Fatima; they shunned the society of just the people whose minds they ought surely to be trying to enlighten. . . ?

"We enlighten minds by contact, yes, but we *pray* for souls—do penance—'this kind goeth not out but by prayer and fasting'. . . ."

The other train thundered relentlessly beside me on its track; it had a heavier engine than mine, an infinitely louder blast on its whistle. "Well, pray and fast then," I advised myself philosophically, and became wholly silent.

We ought to love the world; what was the good of any of us if we were not loving the place and the people we were working for? Why couldn't Elizabeth love the world like anybody else, that is to say by living in it?

In the speaker's opinion, the moment we tried to get away from a thing or a person, we showed that we did not really love them, and if Elizabeth ran away from the world, then she didn't love the world; and God had loved it.

As a matter of fact Elizabeth had by no means run away from the world; on the contrary she had almost crawled backwards out of it, as most of us do, with agonized eyes fixed on its beauty and its appeal until the clang of the heavy convent doors shut it out for ever from her physical vision, and instead drew, with that last hammer-stroke of God, its beauty and its appeal for ever into her soul.

Mystics were misguided Christians who sought to escape all the implications of the Incarnation, and suffered from the dangerous delusions which arose from a complete lack of understanding of Christ's mission upon earth.

And at that moment, by the grace of God, there was a knock at the door. Alarmed by my prolonged absence, a kindly Sister Imelda had sent the postulant to see if I were alive, or whether, by any chance, the lion had somehow managed to scramble through the bars and devour me. " *Deo gratias*," I cried gratefully, and Elizabeth stood before us. But it was an Elizabeth I did not know. Calm, slightly quizzical, unruffled, she surveyed her mother through the grille.

" Hullo, darling! " she exclaimed in a friendly voice. " On the war-path? "

I rose. " I'll leave you together," I murmured and went thankfully towards the door. It was not perhaps the way in which we used to talk to our mothers, but I felt they were best left to converse in a language which presumably they both understood. That one glimpse of the worldly Elizabeth, however, had given me more

realization of the almost incredible effect of the grace of
God in a soul than anything she could have told me in
words. So *that* was Libby, her mother's daughter; and
this was our Sister Elizabeth! I thanked God as I
walked down the corridor. An anxious Sister Imelda
awaited me outside the community-room and handed
me a letter.

"Quite safe?" she enquired solicitously, as she drew
me inside. "The post came while you were in there.
Was she very angry?" I glanced at the Roman post-
mark.

"First there is what those books on the novitiate say;
after that comes what the postulant says; then what her
mother says; and now there is what Monsignor has to
add."

"We might as well be living in the Ring and the
Book, mightn't we?" agreed Sister Imelda, with hazy
recollections of English literature classes floating at the
back of her mind.

"I suppose we had better go and send her lunch outside," was all I said. And even Browning could not have
made a poem out of that.

CHAPTER XIII

THE DOUBTER

B ETWEEN atheism and regretful unbelief there is all the difference in the world; that is what many people do not quite realize. Nevertheless, that which ends in regretful unbelief has often begun in voluntary folly: that is also true. And the folly consists in indiscriminate and risky reading without proper safeguards. Even so great a theologian as Père Garrigou Lagrange once said to some nuns to whom he was giving a conference: "Pray for the theologians—ah, pray for them! They have to read so much, and so much that is unsound. Pray for their faith." And yet, any girl or young man, without special knowledge, without adequate safeguards of any kind, will manage to get a dispensation and begin a course of reading calculated to upset anything but the most solidly grounded principles.

Of course reading is absolutely necessary to intellectual life, and an understanding of the other side of the question is equally essential to any real study of a subject. But the mistake which is so often made by eager youth is to begin at the wrong end. Let us master the whole matter thoroughly first; let us get its foundations and its principles so firmly embedded in our consciousness that no passing opinions to the contrary will lightly affect our view of it. Let us be sure of our answers before the other man begins asking his questions; and do not let us leave our minds for an instant with a vacuum which his doubts may fill.

I

A full mind is the greatest possible safeguard against absorbing too easily another man's theories; just as a good meal is the best possible precaution against stealing someone else's food. But to smell other people's dinners cooking when one has had none oneself is as dangerous to honesty as to listen to other people's ideas on an empty head is dangerous to faith, and that is a fact. Nature always seeks to fill a vacuum, and so, as we value our health and happiness, let us keep our own vacuums filled.

We do not mean to lose our belief in God, that is clear; we have no intention of doing anything wrong or dangerous at all. When we are young we are quite sure that it is a duty to know all about everything; and this particular reading which we are doing happens to come into the everything of our life. Quite possibly that is true, but, once again, let us begin at the right end. When we are older, practical experience is our great safeguard and check; but when we are young we have not that to fall back upon, and we are dependent upon sheer intellectual knowledge. Practical experience has yet to come.

Later on we shall be able to pause as we read of some new and alluring theory of life; with a smile we shall realize that it does not always work out quite like that; that there is this to be said against it; those other probable consequences which have been overlooked. We know better by the first taste and smell of it whether what is offered us is good to eat or not. But that kind of knowledge often comes too late or, at all events, only comes in time to help us to put straight the mistake we have made, but not to prevent our making it.

Dostoyevsky once wrote to a friend about a man who had insulted Christ in his presence: " In insulting Him he has never asked himself, ' Whom are we to put in His place? Ourselves?' Ah, no, he has never thought of that.''[1] Before we give up God so easily, let us reflect instead on whom we shall find to occupy His empty throne. The faith we once had for the asking, now lost, it may take us ten, twenty years to recover: to find out for ourselves that there is no one else. Either it is Christ or we are alone.

But let us be practical. Let us imagine that the mischief has already begun; we have felt the first chill shade of doubt creep into our faith, that easy faith which we have always taken for granted; we have felt for the first time a sinister sensation of distance between God and ourselves; a certain coldness in the air, a mist between us and heaven which chills and frightens. No reading about this experience can induce it: it rises in the soul. It is not catching in itself—unless we deliberately lay ourselves open to infection, carelessly disregarding all precautions. The loss and the return: thank God, there are nearly always those two stages: but it is the years between which hurt.

The worst of it is that the good Catholic, to whom the case is put sometimes in the first beginnings of the perplexities, is so apt to misunderstand. "Behave as if you believed," he says cheerfully, and the wretched sufferer walks away telling himself hopelessly that it is sheerly impossible. His irritation grows as he thinks about it, until finally he is blaming the Church for one man's lack of personal experience. For it is not bad advice in itself, only it needs amplification. He is right in that the crucial mistake which people are apt to make is in acquiescing in the loss, in drifting with the tide instead of turning and swimming resolutely against it from the beginning.

We are speaking here, of course, of the loss of faith,

[1] Letter dated 1871 written to Strachov, quoted in *Dostoyevsky*, by Henri Troyat, 1940, p. 138.

and not of that absence of faith which is due to never having believed. That is the position of the born pagan, but we are thinking now only of the position of the lapsed Christian, Catholic or otherwise. There are those who have never had the Faith and know little more than the name of God; if they are interested at all, they need instruction in the truths of Christianity more than anything else. There are also the determined lapsed Catholics, those strange people who, while they protest that they have never lost the Faith, yet resolutely refuse to practise their religion. For them one can only pray, and trust that when they are dying, they will have time and opportunity—as they will certainly have the desire —to send for a priest.

But the state of which we are speaking is quite other than either of these; a state at once more subtle and infinitely more painful. The initial folly, whatever it was, may have been theirs it is true, but they are now perfectly honest; they quite genuinely believe that they have lost their faith, and yet they know that they did not intentionally lose it. If they went back, they would probably do the same thing again, because they do not see where they went wrong. In a way that is a guarantee of their present sincerity. To them knowledge is only what every intelligent person ought to have: knowledge is knowledge and no one ought to shirk imbibing it because of fear. If it leads them where they do not wish intellectually, that may be a tragedy, but it is not a tragedy of their making. If the path they took led to truth, then they were right to have followed it, however bitter the truth may be.

What they do not see is that all this plausible reasoning comes after the apparent loss of faith. What were they doing before? One thing is absolutely certain beyond a shadow of doubt. If anyone is in possession of the love and the knowledge of Christ; if anyone has absolutely absorbed the teaching of the Gospels; has followed the ministry and the passion of Our Lord, and watched Him heal the sick, feed the hungry, deal tenderly with the widow; if anyone has seen Christ's own reactions to pain, to suffering, to love and to sin; has been with Him at the Last Supper and listened to His tender exhortations, and stood at the foot of the cross and watched Him die; has stared with Peter and John into the empty tomb and known the joy of the first meeting with the risen Lord: he is in possession of Truth itself and he need fear no other.

Now he may go out into the world and do modest battle for the Master whom he serves. Incarnate Faith accompanies him, and so long as he keeps in that company he is safe. But that was the initial folly which he made; that was the foolishness which unwittingly he did. His danger began when he went out into the world without Christ, trusting in his own brain, his own powers of discrimination to guide him; when he set out in pursuit of the knowledge of men, *without first having made sure of the knowledge of God*; when he thought to grow wise and be able to argue with others before he had learned all that there was need for him to know of God.

During the years in the wilderness when he does not perceive all this, there is little that others can do but to pray. The return must begin with the one who wandered. But any one of us might be the cause of that beginning. We can never know what will touch his soul; what fortuitous encounter, what passing words almost casually uttered, may be the first step for him of the great return. Only God knows, who gives the grace, and the happy soul who takes it.

Of the return itself there is little to say because there is too much to say. Each soul will set out upon the home-journey differently. In the story which Douglas Hyde has told in his moving narrative *I Believed*, is shown a way back (for Douglas Hyde had been a Methodist and an embryo minister before ever he was a Communist) which, although it is unique and utterly personal, is nevertheless also characteristic of returns in general.[2]

First there were the long months of doubt and agony, the false steps, the hesitations: the ceaseless arguments with self, while the more recent habits beat against the old faith and the half-forgotten practices of long ago. And then finally, just in one amazing moment, everything co-ordinated and the impossible accomplished by the dimly-remembered words of a popular song of twenty years before.

Everyone knows the story of St. Etheldreda's; of the little Irish girl who went to light a candle to Our Lady, and in lighting it lit a flame in the soul of Douglas Hyde; of how, when she had gone, after he had seen her face— her face as she went up to speak to Our Lady and her face as she came back—in an act of blind faith he copied each of her actions. He too went up the aisle, put his pennies in the box, lit his candle, and tried to pray. And the prayer, which at last in despair he used, and which finally gave him back the lost treasure of his belief in God, had nothing at all to do with anything but his own soul. It was just, as he tells us, the words of a song of which he had once bought a gramophone record when he was young. But they were sufficient for Our Lady, who, when all is said and done, had waited for Douglas Hyde much longer than he had waited for her.

I always remember a conversation to which I listened one day sitting up on the Pincio above Rome. It was between two charming young people, both of whom had managed to lapse away from their religion. We sat on

[2] *I Believed*. Douglas Hyde. p. 258.

the parapet, looking over the lovely view of roofs towards Monte Mario in the distance, while the dome
of St. Peter's stood out bold and uncompromising
against the blue of the May sky. If ever a conversation
were inappropriate in its setting, that conversation was.

The girl stared at St. Peter's with a slight frown; then
she looked at the priest; then finally at her companion.
The priest, friendly then as he still is now, to young
people, and to their problems and decisions, smiled back
at her, half quizzically.

"There he is," she cried, pointing at him, "sitting
on his side of the ditch, and here are we on ours. If you
saw someone in the ditch between us, Michael, just
exactly in the middle, trying to get out, which side should
you pull him out on—his or ours?" Michael did not
answer. She shook an accusing finger at the priest:
"Which is the happier, he or we, tell me that!" she
said.

Michael looked towards the horizon with half-closed
eyes as though the better to focus his thoughts, and he
spoke slowly.

"If they were the least bit on his side, and if I thought
they could get out alone, I should leave them to get out.
But if they were exactly in the middle and I saw that they
could not scramble out by themselves, I should"—he
hesitated and flushed a little—"I should pull them out
on ours."

She nodded. "And *you*," she demanded, turning to
the priest, "what would you do? Pull them out on your
side whatever they wanted I suppose?" It was rude,
but the dome of St. Peter's was visibly getting on her
nerves.

"No," he said, shaking his head.

"What then?"

"If I *pulled* them out—which I don't suppose I could

—and they did not want to come, they would only go back. What would be the good of that?"

"Oh, don't be so placid!" she stormed.

"I have everything to be placid about," he reminded her.

"What would you *do*? You couldn't just sit and watch."

"No," he said, "and neither could God. If they had nice, open minds like you and Michael"—she winced —"and if they were as fair as he is and as unbitter, which is the test of sincerity. . . ." They stared at each other in the hot sunlight and neither of them would give way.

"Well?" she said at last.

"It was you who spoke of the middle of the ditch," he went on smoothly, "and it is to the middle of the ditch that I am sticking. Argument is no use—only makes people angry"—she bit her lip while he watched Michael blowing smoke-rings from his cigarette—"I should know that sooner or later God would give them the grace and courage to see their mistakes and scramble up again by themselves. Michael said that, not I," he added blandly.

"Oh!" she cried in furious protest, but he waved her aside and went on. Michael himself said nothing.

"The closed mind is the real barrier to the return," he said, getting up firmly. "God never forces the will, but if we are really looking for truth, I think we shall always find it."

That priest had a way of being right then, so many years ago, as he still has now. It was not, I think, so very long, before they did.

CHAPTER XIV

ENGAGEMENT

SISTER Imelda appeared suddenly round the bushes; her face was distressed. " Are you very busy? " she asked deprecatingly. " Because, if you are not, Marigold has had a stroke."

I was relieved that it was only Marigold; after all, it might have been one of us. Nevertheless I followed hastily to the fowlhouse, and there, sure enough, was Marigold in her nest in a recumbent position but apparently quite comfortable. She regarded us politely, without speaking.

" It has only taken her in her legs," explained Sister Imelda, " You can see—her mind is quite clear."

" Yet it seems to have affected her speech," I remarked with regrettable frivolity.

" Oh—o-o-o! " said Marigold suddenly, putting her head on one side. It gave me quite a shock.

" What's the matter, old lady," I went on, administering .a discreet poke, " come along now, upsey-daisy! " Marigold however firmly declined to upsey-daisy or anything else. She sat perfectly still and stared at us unwinkingly. " Perhaps she is broody? Perhaps she is going to moult? Perhaps she is going to lay an egg? " I now felt that I had explored every possible avenue of explanation, and prepared to return to my work.

" But she has laid once already this morning," objected Sister Imelda, catching desperately at our habit.

" Perhaps she is going to lay twice then—one never

know what your fowls may be going to do." Whenever anything goes wrong, I notice, there is a general tendency to regard the chickens as belonging exclusively to Sister Imelda. On other occasions, of course, they belong to us all.

There was a day, for instance, last summer when Anthony had to come and tell us that Caritas was in the pond. He searched the garden, and when at last he found us, ran backwards and forwards, turned repeated somersaults, tried everything in fact except transforming himself into a dog and barking, before he managed to convince us that something was wrong. Ultimately we were obliged to follow as he led the way, and there, sure enough, sitting in the middle of the miniature pond, supported by a tuft of clotted grass and water-lily root, was Caritas. The water lapped her draggled tail, the water oozed up through her sodden breast feathers, it rippled and gurgled all round her, as she clung despairingly to her small island. Anthony sat down at the edge and surveyed her caustically.

"Silly thing," he said, as plain as a cat could, and immediately began to wash himself; possibly by way of demonstrating that it is perfectly simple to take a satisfactory bath without sitting on a water-lily in the middle of a lake to do it. We got her out with ladders and things, and Sister Imelda put her on the kitchen boiler to dry—upon which she immediately laid an egg, whether by gratitude or delayed shock we were unable to decide.

"Well, fancy that!" said Sister Imelda picking it up, "After all this, she must be feeling a little weak. I will fetch her some Parrish's Food." Now of Parrish's Food we have plenty, thanks to our hermit's foresight. When, some time ago, we were warned of an approaching shortage of iron and steel, she was asked, as general gardener and carpenter, to send out and buy whatever she thought we might need in that way before it was too late. I was a little mystified to find six large bottles of tonic added to the list. "But you *said* shortage of iron," protested Sister Imelda, quite hurt.

It was after that, of course, that she also became so very interested in salvage: so interested in fact that the sisters had to take to polishing hard in order to save their most cherished possessions from the dustman. The least sign of rust settled the question for Sister Imelda, if not for the owner. She seized every ancient tool and for-gotten spade that she could lay hands upon. When I asked her if she really thought that such dilapidated objects could be of any use for recasting, she assured me earnestly that they most certainly could.

"It is like conversion," she explained, "the most unlikely people and even vessels of wrath turned into shining examples of sanctity and virtue. They will take your old spade and melt it down into a beautiful new weapon of defence—a spear for instance."

"Oh, thank you," I said politely, "that will be most useful."

When we returned to Marigold half an hour later, she was sitting happily upon her second egg, and even seemed determined to hatch it out before dinner-time.

"There—tut—tut—all that fuss for nothing," cried Sister Imelda, apparently forgetting for the moment who had made the fuss. "Why ever didn't you say that that was all it was?"

Whether it be due to the iron in Parrish's Food, or to love of Sister Imelda, I do not know, but certainly our fowls will lay for her as surely fowls never laid before. Once indeed, when two bishops announced themselves suddenly for lunch, plus their retinues, and we had only two eggs in all the world, they rose to the occasion as one hen.

"You can't offer two eggs to two bishops," said I in despair.

Sister Imelda wasted no time in lamentations. She fetched an empty altar-wine bottle, filled it with hot water, and put it in a nest of straw. She then seized the likeliest looking fowl and sat her down upon it. "Lay, Bird, lay," she commanded, while she fed her with special tit-bits. After a period of astonishment, Bird settled down to it. The grateful warmth rose in her feathers. "O——o-o-o" she murmured softly, "go away, I'm busy."

Sister Imelda shut down the door of the nest and on tip-toe we retreated. The other fowls stood round and watched, particularly when it came to the titbits. We noticed that they looked thoughtful. During the next hour a strange peace brooded over the fowl-run; not a sound was to be heard, not a cackle, not a rustle of up-turned leaves.

"Whatever is the matter with them all?" cried Sister Imelda at last, and went to look. She came back with a gratified countenance and fifteen eggs. So in the end it was bishops we ran short of.

Our hens are evidently fully 'engaged' in their life's work, and any Existentialist might be proud of them. On the other hand, their obedience is most edifying, so that they seem to reflect two of the principal topics of discussion to-day. For the modern *culte* for freedom and independence has naturally led to an equal interest in its opposite quality, that is to say obedience, regarded either as a virtue or a vice, and in particular religious obedience, as the high-water mark of all obedience. It has been dealt with from almost every point of view, but mainly, of course, from either the theological or psychological angle.

There still remains, however, an extensive region of

thought on the subject not very fully dealt with, and that region is as interesting to the secular as to the religious, to the woman as to the man, since it is concerned directly with the will of God, which is, after all, the affair of all Christians whatever their particular state in life. It is just the ordinary, practical view of it: the sort of view which we take in everyday affairs, without going too precisely into the dogma of our decisions. The ordinary woman has not much time to dogmatize as she goes about the day's business, but she can always love the will of God, whatever her occupations.

The acceptance of the will of God, either directly or through the expressed will of another in authority, is always a meritorious act; but in order to bring our view of it into line with the modern way of thinking, with for instance the Existentialist exaltation of *engagement* and freedom, it must have a far broader basis than mere acceptance. Let *us* also engage ourselves to do God's will, to love it, to work for it. The main reason for the explicit vow made by the religious, is just that he (or she) is so determined not to do his own will, that he engages to accept the will of another, and to act according to it, on all legitimate occasions. Freedom is safeguarded, because the choice is the choice of the person making the vow, yet it is active and forceful enough, surely, to satisfy even the most ardent desire for definite living as opposed to drifting.

Obviously people living in the world, apart from members of the Secular Institutes, cannot go to quite these lengths, but those who are aiming at spiritual perfection, just as the Existentialist is aiming at psychological perfection, can engage themselves equally to accept the will of God wherever it is plainly manifest, that is to say in matters over which they have no direct control, and to act in accordance with it. Further, they can engage to choose for themselves, whenever there are two courses open to them, the one in which there appears to be more of God's will. This precludes the deliberate choice of any course which involves, in however slight a degree, actual sin, or even grave imperfection. It is indeed a mild form of the vow of the most perfect advocated by St. Teresa of Avila.

Thus the Christian, whether secular or religious, can feel himself to be no less engaged, no less enterprising, to be risking no less in the determined pursuit of God's will, than say the Existentialist or the Communist in the determined pursuit of his own.

In the end we always come back to the simple fact that just because the original Fall of man was due to disobedience, the ultimate return to God must be by obedience also: and that, in spite of sin, in spite of human weakness and disorder, this return is still open to mankind. It is open to each man and therefore it is open to all men.

As things are, the likelihood of its being accepted, even as a principle, by mankind in general, is certainly remote, but the solid fact remains that, in spite of the Fall and all its bitter consequences: consequences widening and deepening with every succeeding generation: were all men and women to begin to act now in accordance with what appeared to them genuinely to be the will of God, a certain wide harmony would return to the earth as a result. It is true that the diversity of interpretations of the will of God would at first be quite staggering, particularly among the feminine portion of creation, but that would adjust itself by degrees, and at all events it would be clear from the very beginning that no one could venture to interpret the will of God as involving anything in itself bad.

Such dreams as these belong to that wonderful land

called Utopia; but then so also do the dreams of the
Communists or pagan Existentialists, or any other purely
ideological dreams. Even the Existentialists, although
they call themselves by that name, cannot really exist
altogether satisfactorily in the world which they have
built, for the very simple reason that it does not exist,
in their form, for the rest of us. To live in a world of
your own is all very well up to a certain point, but it is
not very practical. The Communist is in the same difficulty: his wonderful, material world, in which he is
going to be so happy one day when it has become a paradise, is constantly being upset, his dream is always being
shattered, by the impact of a force which, as a matter of
fact, he does not admit: a spiritual force. He gnashes
his teeth, and goes on ramming with all his material
resources, all the human strength which he can gather
together, at something which constantly eludes him, constantly disappears as he slays it, and reappears in unexpected places when he thought it long since dead.

The Christian bases his faith on the truth of this
world, on the fact that it is the world which God made,
and that the plan behind it is God's plan and not the
plan of any man. However much human wisdom there
may be in the pagan philosophies, they, and the worlds
which they would create, are only based on the thoughts
of finite intellects; but the Christian's world is not actually *based* on anything at all. It is conceived and wholly
contained within the infinite power and knowledge of
God. That is the difference between our Christian
world—this world in which we so truly live, and hope,
and act—and all the other conceptions of the world which
have sprung from the imagination of man.

So, in God's world, which is our world by His gift, we
Christians, wherever we happen to be and whatever our
occupation, can make His will the passion of our lives.

Yet there are necessarily degrees in the practical application of any intellectually accepted principle. Just as there are philosophers, and there are Communists and pagan Existentialists, who devote the whole of their time and energy to the spread of their respective doctrines, and there are mere dilettantes whose adherence to the creed of their choice is largely theoretical and a matter of leisure moments, while other interests form the real centre of life for them; so we shall find, in our case, the same thing in the pursuit of the will of God. There is every degree of fervour to be met with, from its passive acceptance without complaint when it is inescapable (but, one must admit, a tendency to struggle against it with considerable vigour when it is not!) up to the joyous and total gift of self practised by the saints.

Some self-chosen circumstances in life, indeed, would seem to make the determined and active pursuit of the will of God very difficult of realization. Take the case of a woman who marries a man who is not a Catholic and has no intention of becoming one. (He may yet become one, it is true, but she has no right whatsoever to count upon it.) How can she later impose on him as a ground for some joint action which faces them—this course or that?—the argument of the over-riding importance of following the will of God, and of doing nothing contrary to it? His answer will naturally be: "Who says that it is the will of God, anyway?" And when she tells him who says it, he will smile politely at the mention of an authority whom he does not acknowledge.

Again, there is the girl who of choice, and not of necessity, takes work beyond the reach of a Catholic church. It may be true that, once she is settled there, distance absolves her from her duty to attend Mass on Sunday; it may also be true that it is an excellent post which no sensible girl could be expected to decline. Maybe. Still, let us be realistic enough to acknowledge that this is not the sort of ardour which is going to defeat Communism, make a stand against the arguments of pagan Existentialism, and convert the world.

Such Christians may indeed save their souls but they are not very likely to help to save any others. The most that can be said of them is that they do no harm, and even that is not altogether true because tepidity always does this much harm: it spreads a faint, grey haze over everything, which obscures the view and dulls down even the brightest colours. Here is the Church of Christ in all her glory, and here are the ardent, apostolic Christians of the world in all their numbers. But both the glory and the numbers are apt to be hidden from the sight of the outsider, of the casual observer, by the drifting mist of indifference which hangs round the outer edge of Christendom, and the dreary wanderers to be met with in its outskirts.

It is all very negative, but that is just what both the Communist and the pagan Existentialist seize upon and exploit to the full. Each in his own way calls upon youth to be positive—to engage itself—to take life's risks and live at the heart of things. That challenge is simple enough to answer, but only if we accept it and take it up in the name of the Church. She too calls upon youth to follow, to be positive, and to take upon itself fearlessly the glorious risks, if such we care to call them, of living, not at the heart of things, but at the Heart of Christ Himself.

K

CHAPTER XV

LIBERTY AND LICENCE

W E quoted in an earlier chapter the comprehensive definition of Existentialism suggested by Roger Troisfontaines: " Existentialism is a passionate return by the individual to his liberty in an attempt to discover, from the unfolding of his own conduct, the meaning of his existence." He explains later in detail exactly what he understands by this. The new creed is, in effect, a revolt of the individual against those philosophies which tend to absorb personal originality into the abstraction of a system. The man who is passionately interested in living, and who has only one life to live, grows impatient with the dreamy observer of the universal. He is concerned solely with the concrete *Me*.

Personal liberty is the fetish, therefore, of the Existentialist, and the origin of all his entirely subjective values. If he misses the wider view of the idealist, at least he does his best to give his own interpretation to the world as he sees it. And very queerly indeed he sees it at times. A world without God, the Creator; a world without Christ, the Redeemer; a strange and depressing world in truth. An impossible world, because it could not in fact exist, although the Existentialist is under the impression that he lives in it. It takes one back to Setebos:

> " Setebos, Setebos, and Setebos!
> Thinketh, he dwelleth i' the cold o' the moon "

and apparently the Existentialist thinketh that he dwelleth in it along with him.

According to him, the only means of arriving at the truth is by personal experience. We must live to know life. No intellectual representation of truth will give us the truth itself: the whole of it for each of us is contained in the changing circumstances and acts of our existence: truth *is* no more, in fact, than truth-as-we-see-it.

The one solidly good thing about Existentialism is that it is in complete opposition to all forms of Totalitarianism. Father Copleston, S.J., while he does not suggest that it is a conscious reaction against Marxism, yet says that it is possibly " to be partially explained as a reaction against modern collectivistic and totalitarian trends ".[1] However that may be, we cannot get away from the fact that, as again pointed out by Roger Troisfontaines,[2] if oppressed, or even if only suffering from a feeling of oppression, the man of action will react by organizing either resistance or revolution; but, strangely enough, our Existentialist is not himself primarily a man of action, and the poet, the dreamer, the introspective, reacts only mentally and emotionally. He expresses himself in what one might call an excess of personal individuality; he refuses to be swept intellectually into a stream, he stoutly declines to be absorbed into the mass.

It may be this which lies at the root of the extreme individualism of the Existentialist. The speculative study of his liberty becomes an absorbing passion, and, the more absorbing, the more he retreats from any attempt to systematize either himself or his surroundings. Freewill is his principal pre-occupation, but *acts* of freewill are usually unpredictable, therefore they cannot be

---

[1] *Existentialism and Modern Man.* F. C. Copleston, S.J. p. 11.
[2] *Existentialisme et Pensée Chrétienne.* Troisfontaines. p. 94 etc.

deduced by reason and must be lived to be understood. Thus those things which are observable; which can be experienced, tasted, felt; become the only things by which he believes that he can safely judge. His idea is not to lay down laws in regard to life, but to consider situations and events, or states of mind, which have been definitely lived and experienced, and to search for their explanation while, if possible, finding a solution for them.

This worship of liberty, as a thing in itself, is certainly not confined to the followers of the new philosophy. It is the positive idol of the greater number of the present generation, although in the homage which they pay to it they are not so very original when all is said and done. Freedom of conscience, of nations, of speech, of elections, of government, are freedoms which we ought all to love; but so often the practice of individual freedom merely degenerates into a doing of what we know we ought not to do, just because we happen to want to do it. Nobody is going to lose his life for that sort of freedom. It is quite possible to lose both health and spiritual sanity on account of it—but not in the grand manner.

Most of the avowed Existentialists who have, as they imagine, tasted life, have found that it is not so sweet after all, but almost sickeningly absurd. They find even the sensation of liberty, which when rightly enjoyed is to the rest of us one of the most inspiring and sustaining sensations in the world, only a further source of anguish because, since there is nothing for them worth while in life: no values which in themselves are noble enough to attract the will: they are, as Heidegger and the more extreme of the French leaders express it, lost in the void, "comme perdue dans le néant".

They have at last, however, grasped the conclusions of a negative philosophy as opposed to the classical philosophy of affirmation. They have finally emphasized for us this truth: if we cannot find, or do not seek to find, a real *raison d'être* for our presence in this world, then immediately we become aware, to a greater or lesser degree according to our capacity for interior reflection, that we are in danger of being stifled by a sensation of nausea, futility, and mental suffering.

The three great values recognized by traditional philosophy are Truth, Beauty and Goodness. If we deny Truth we are faced with absurdity and futility: nothing is solid, everything which we encounter resolves itself into no more than a mask to hide the emptiness behind it. If we deny Beauty, we taste the nausea of a drab and monotonous world. If we deny Goodness, then in the end we are faced with anguish of the soul—for the soul, although we may deny its existence with our lips and with our pretended intellect, we cannot deny with our Being, which is itself.

The interesting thing about consciousness, that great factor in the thought of the Existentialists, is that it is not only a matter of the present moment. What complicates life for us is that it exists also in the past and in the future. I am actually conscious of the present moment, but I am also conscious of the past by memory and of the future by imagination. As a matter of fact, thought only becomes conscious thought by drawing back, as it were, a little from itself. Père Grevillot, in elaborating the current theory of consciousness, personal responsibility, and liberty of action, quotes the saying of Hegel: " That which appears to me as myself—my Being—is that which I have just been ".[3]

By becoming past, our conscious acts are not destroyed, neither are they separated from us in order to sink into oblivion, for the effect of them continues to exist as part

[3] *Les Grands Courants de la Pensée Contemporaine.* Grevillot. p. 42.

of the structure of our Being, by means of which we can define ourselves clearly. This is, of course, according to the accepted Catholic teaching, and it is interesting to note how strongly the Existentialists insist on this fact of the continued presence of the past, although they draw from it conclusions very different to those of our happy religion. "I am," they say, "having been."

For them, an event which is recalled is as existent as when it happened; it is entirely present—but it is present in the past. This survival of the past is, however, no obstacle to freedom, for it is in the present, at this very moment, that we are judging of that past, and so determining our future. It is in the present, at this very moment, in effect, that we decide whether such and such an act of yesterday were good or bad, to be repeated or to be condemned. We continue triumphantly free in all our acts, because the past can only influence the present according to the sense which we ourselves choose to give to it. We are free to continue along the lines of yesterday's action, or we can forsake that course altogether in order to follow a different one. "The future is that which I have to be to the extent that I am able not to be it": a subtle saying no doubt, and not altogether untrue.

But there are degrees in the Existentialist's freedom, or at all events degrees of the extent to which he uses it. The effect of the past upon the future is a matter of delicate balance and, according to him, we are therefore only truly and perfectly free if we direct the whole of our future in the light and by the functioning of the whole of our past. Nothing of life should be wasted: no emotion, no sensation, no experience. But it is a very strange and eerie world in which the Existentialist lives, none the less. It reminds one a little of an Arthur Wrackham drawing.

" In the present he is, in effect, a living knowledge and consciousness of things which are exterior to himself: he is his own past as though no longer being it: his future as not yet being it, and able never to be it." For all their claim to the experience of life itself, and to actuality, this is surely the language of the dreamer and the lotus-eater. " He is always separated from that which he is, by the enormous extent of the Being which he is not." Which, in plain English, I take to mean that, as our past and our future have each of them a far greater extent than the actual flash of this present moment in which we are living, Man is, indeed, that " creature of distances " which Heidegger so nostalgically calls him.

But even if he is, I see no cause for hysteria. He has his memory and he has his hopes, and surely no one would be so mad as to want to experience, second by second, more than we already do? God has tempered the extent of our joy and of our pain to our capacity to bear them; and the means He has used are time and space, whereby we receive only what we can manage of either, trickle by trickle. If the Existentialist is wistful and hurt because he cannot have all life to endure at once, he is welcome to his agony of regret: the rest of us are quite satisfied with the amount we receive as things are.

The conscious self can only be a creature of Time, we are told again, because it is perpetually seeking to escape from itself, surging beyond itself, projecting itself. The conscious self is further a lonely thing, enclosed in the void. A sad, a melancholy picture, yet with a certain wistful charm highly dangerous to the wistfully-minded. And in these days of prevalent emptiness, there are many such.

Liberty can be viewed from two angles: either as its own supreme end, and this is the angle of the atheist

Existentialist, or as the necessary condition of an even higher end. The value of Existentialism as a philosophy surely rests on the true answer to that question, for liberty depends for its worth entirely on the use made of it. Gold, for instance, has an intrinsic value of its own, and no matter what temporary use we may make of it, retains that value. Spend it, save it, lose it—it is still worth what it is worth unless we utterly destroy it.

It is not so as regards freedom. That is an individual thing, useful only to ourselves. If we lose our liberty, no one else can find it and profit thereby; it is just so much less freedom in the world unless we personally manage to regain it. Liberty is, in itself, neither good nor bad; its whole value, whether positive or negative, depends upon the use which we make of it.

With this we come to the real crux of the matter. The Existentialist theory of liberty is dangerous because it has a seductive appearance of boldness and initiative. A supreme consciousness of liberty of action implies an obligation to use it: to make of life something positive and worth while. The idea has its attractions, especially to youth looking round, as it were, as we all do when we are young, for something in which to believe profoundly and for which to live. The greatest present danger surely lies in the nebulous position of many Existentialists and their potential disciples as regards Faith, and the vagueness of the line which separates atheist from theist Existentialism.

The fact is that no pagan or atheistic philosophy is really dangerous until we begin to talk about a Catholic form of it. Then it is. To affirm his absolute independence is the constant aim of the Existentialist: this places him above the law and, as Monterlant has said, leads logically in the end to the commission of crime. Liberty thus conceived, which is the sense in which Nietzsche conceived it, is the affirmation of total independence—and therefore of inevitable revolt against God.

The liberty of the Christian is something completely different. It is the affirmation of a God-given gift: free-will. It is also an acknowledgment of the fact that, in the end, God will require an account of the use of that gift. The whole argument of atheistic Existentialism is that man's liberty is supreme and that he owes no allegiance to anyone but himself, and his own self-created values. God is eliminated altogether. It is difficult for the ordinary person to see how there can be a Christian—or even a merely theist—form of such a philosophy. There are points of accord in all philosophies, even the most widely divergent, but if those philosophies reach totally different conclusions as to life, and particularly as to the source of life, can they reasonably be called by the same name?

Kierkegaard, Jaspers and Marcel all admit the transcendent; Sartre denies it; Heidegger is reported to have said that he " does not deny God, but states his absence." Incidentally he dissociates himself from Sartre. Gabriel Marcel has also, of course, definitely repudiated the name " Existentialism" as far as his philosophy is concerned, and prefers that of " Neo-Socratism",—"an attitude of interrogation that is a constant with me" he mildly explains.[1] Taken as a whole, the new philosophy appears to be largely a philosophy of disassociation.

Meanwhile Christianity, it need scarcely be pointed out, is the precise opposite of all this. Its leaders are agreed, because they are all followers of the one supreme leader about whom there is no ambiguity. Christ in us, and we in Christ, and all of us in the Father.

[1] *Metaphysical Journal.* Gabriel Marcel. Translated by Bernard Wall.

CHAPTER XVI

THE CAUSE

SISTER Imelda and the novices were listening to the reading of a book in the garden on a summer feast-day. Anthony who, although he has long since placed himself upon our Chapter and elected himself to our Council, regards himself also as an honorary member of the novitiate, in virtue of his general office of keeping an eye on things, sat in the middle of the flagged semi-circle, while we all sat round on the curved stone seat. Sister Imelda was sticking little pictures on to holy cards and licking the backs of them thoughtfully; the others were either sewing or busy with embroidery, and at intervals, I regret to say, licked their cotton; Anthony, who does not either sew or paint, licked himself.

The book was *The Mass in Slow Motion* by Ronald Knox, and the long green shadows of the branches above made the prettiest patterns at our feet. The particular part we had come to was about Absolom and, striking upon the shimmering, heat-laden air, one could almost hear the snapping of the dry twigs, the beat of the horse's hoofs.

"Some think this was written by King David when he fled from Absolom . . . then there was a battle in which David's men got the better of the revolutionaries, but whether he really wrote this psalm I don't know. It talks about 'the God who gives me the gladness of youth'; King David at the time of Absolom's revolt was getting on for sixty, and you don't feel much joy of youth when you are getting on for sixty. So some people think that the author . . ."

Slowly we became aware of laughter through the sunlight. Delicious laughter reminding one of a child's first unexpected encounter with a joke. There was surprise in it and delight; Sister Imelda, indeed, was shaking like an old-fashioned party jelly, the sort made with a jellybag, her face crinkled with smiles.

"You don't feel much joy of youth when you are getting on for sixty—oh, *don't* you! " The novices joined in the laughter affectionately. "Don't you! What a lovely surprise is waiting for him—dear Monsignor, he is not old enough yet to know! "

What Sister Imelda is not old enough to know, of course, and never will be, is that she has a special secret of her own for happiness, which she learnt straight from God when she was young and has never lost, and that it is a secret mostly hidden from the rest of us, though not, one feels sure, from Ronald Knox. There are ways of living, and ways of living, and on the secrets we learn and absorb as we go through life depends our outlook in old age. Certainly Monsignor Knox need not fear that his *joie de vivre* is likely to fail him, and when he is much more than sixty, he will still, please God, be sharing it with us.

When it comes to living the right way and the wrong way from the eternity point of view, roughly speaking one might say that there are two wrong ways and one right. There is the completely pagan way; and there is the self-indulgent Christian way; and there is the right way, straight for God. That is the way of the saints, but it is our way too if we have any sense.

It is interesting to observe, in the case of good pagans, how strong a sense of eternity still often survives in them, even though ostensibly they are only living for time.

They talk, for instance, as if they would go on for ever: one would almost say that they know, subconsciously, that they will go on for ever: and so they behave, like children burying their heads under the bedclothes in the darkness, as if they could somehow go on living without end here on earth. True, they speak of death as the final close of everything, but in their planning there is always a slurring over of the close for them. It seems as though it were a theoretical end only in which they believe, while deep in their souls persists another and stronger conviction and the haunting desire for everlasting life.

When it comes to Christians there are a dozen different ways of living, not exactly wrongly, but just not quite rightly for eternity. It is a case of thinking and acting along the lines of an almost double existence: an existence in the immediate present for time, and another in the future for eternity, instead of one life lived for God alone, both now and then. The present and future are joined together as one whole, after all, however much we may try to disguise the fact from ourselves.

One day a brilliant and admirable Catholic gave me an almost bitter little estimate of his own life, made when he felt that he was nearing the end of it. He was not at the end of it by any means, but the end was, I suppose, sufficiently in sight to give him a fresh view of earth. He told me that, on looking at the particular shelf which contained his own books—for he was an intellectual—he picked out the latest, glanced at it, and flung it aside, saying to himself: " and on such worthless trifles I have wasted my life ".

" But . . ." I cried, for trifles is certainly not the word which most of his admirers would apply to his works.

" There is no ' but ' when it comes to God. I see now

that one lives for earth or one lives for heaven, and I, like a fool, have lived for earth."

"But . . ."

"Oh, granted, with one eye on heaven perhaps. But that does not do it. Not when one comes within close sight of heaven, and earth lies behind."

I cried no more buts, because I knew that he was right. He was sad, now that old age was upon him, not because of age itself but because of the youth and prime which had gone before it. If we grow old in the wrong way, it is perhaps because we were young in the wrong way too. It is not that there is any need for us to fly from the world: indeed that is not even desirable in most cases since the world must perforce go on: but, nevertheless, whilst living a perfectly normal life, we can still live it according to God's will and not according to our own. To say that the two wills can usually be made to coincide is not quite true—unless, indeed, we mean that we intend to force our own to coincide with God's on every occasion. But that, one is obliged to admit, is not usually the manner in which the coincidence shows itself.

If we do not actively oppose God's will, and there are many good Christians who would not dream of con- sciously doing such a thing, yet we can altogether miss God's will; pass it by in our blindness as though, for us, it did not exist; and the consequences of that blindness may fall upon others as well as ourselves. God will never allow us ultimately to over-ride any purpose of His; the plan which we have spoilt for the moment by our selfish unawareness will, if it were His plan, certainly be carried out in the end. Still, this is not the sort of co-operation with God's will which is going to help save the world in its twentieth-century difficulties.

"And who is to know that it *was* God's will and God's plan?" you exclaim.

Who indeed? But at least we can know this much:
that it was not ours, and so might well be His. And, on
the contrary, of these plans of our own upon which
we set our minds so resolutely, we might well say that
they are so obviously ours that they might easily be no
one else's. There is a very great safety in not doing our
own will, particularly in those cases where we have a
strong urge to do it. Let us wait first and see if others
urge us also. Usually they do not.

A very simple way of judging for ourselves whether we
are prepared to follow God's will is to notice whether
we have any, what might be called, violent currents in
our thoughts. "*I could not do that.*" If it is a sin of
which we are speaking, or an imperfection, or a folly—
well and good: but in such a case do not let us be
too sure that we could not do it. If, on the contrary, it
is merely some blameless course of action to which we
personally object, then we have all the ingredients ready
to hand for a refusal of God's will. For who is to know
whether that very course may not one day be God's
special request of us? In the same way: "I simply must
do so and so" is never good, even if the thing in question is not only harmless but even admirable: for there
is no "simply must" in the following of God's will. It is
always and only a humble treading in His footsteps, a
peaceful waiting for each movement of His, no matter
whether it be a beckoning or a waving-back.

There remains the right way of living, straight for
God. That is a life of selfless devotion, wherever it may
be lived. But, in trying to live in such a way, we have to
beware lest we look for results in time. When we choose
this path we are living for eternity, and only in eternity
will the little tree of our love flower and show its fruit.
We are, in a sense, following a vision, living for an ideal,
and when we do this on earth there is always the pos-

sibility of the disaster of personal disillusionment. Yet, if we are wise, if we remain unruffled under all circumstances, if we truly desire only the glory of God, there is the simplest way of avoiding any such tragedy: for disillusionment is always a tragedy.

In any work undertaken for God, let us keep the Cause itself, and the individuals connected with it, separate in our minds. It is the Cause itself which matters, which enthralls, which arouses the selfless devotion. The individuals who are inevitably connected with it, and so with us, are only incidental. It is true that, if such is the case, then they may also regard us as incidental. By all means! It is our very great privilege, and theirs, to be joined together in this or that plan for the glory of God. But it is also a fact that if we, and they, were not there to carry out the plan, it would still be carried out: provided that it is really a plan dear to the heart of God. God can dispense with you and me in the carrying out of His designs. To say, or to allow others to say, that we are indispensable, is to say that the work we are doing is not God's work but ours. If it be His work He can find plenty of tools with which to finish it. Let us labour humbly, live without exaggeration, knowing that we are never irreplaceable; and so shall we safely avoid all danger of disillusion.

There was a certain Sheik on the Persian Gulf in whose territory oil was found, and who thus became as fabulously rich as any Prince in the *Arabian Nights*. A deeply religious man, his one idea was to use his newly found wealth in improving the standards of living for the people of his small territory. Among other things, he proposed to rebuild the chief city. That was his vision and that the lifework which he set himself and, in its own way, it was conceived and undertaken for the love of God—his God.

Now that would not alter the fact that when he came to carry it out, he would most probably meet with the usual Mrs. Smiths and Mrs. Joneses who never like what other people are building for them. If a house has been decided upon with two sitting-rooms and three bedrooms, Mrs. Smith will wish that it had been one living-room and four bedrooms, she having a large family; Mrs. Jones will think it too large altogether, she having a small one; and Mrs. Brown will probably say that she quite likes it except for the shape of the roof. Our vision is in danger of being shattered by details and personalities. But let us still hold it closely to our heart. There will always be a Mrs. Smith in every earthly vision, and we must not forget that we are probably as much of a calamity to her as she is to us.

In spite of us both the vision persists; it is something which will endure long after we are dead. For we, and our Mrs. Smiths and Browns, are only passing, as far as earth is concerned. It is true that the planning —in Time and under God—is undertaken for the benefit of those very Browns and Smiths, and for the benefit of whole generations of them. But let us console ourselves. The generations will get the benefit, if we are patient and persevering, whatever the individual Smiths and Browns think about it—and think about us.

Let us keep our ideal, which is a little piece of God's plan, and live for it; we shall be happy. Let us bear with Mrs. Smith too, and we shall be still happier—whatever Mrs. Smith is.

The ideal, the cause, goes on and grows with every faithful generation. In spite of all the Mrs. Smiths in the world, the trend is upwards.

So we come back to Monsignor Knox and the slow-motion of his mass, and we shall see that it is the same for all life. We live—we receive life—in slow motion: in details, one by one. Yet through it all, and above it all, there surges the rush and the force and the overwhelming grace of God's love, and of His mercy and forgiveness poured out on the foolish generations of men.

L

CHAPTER XVII

THE EXISTENTIALIST AND THE CHRISTIAN

IT is quite clear that the main thing which we are fighting in our spiritual war is atheistic philosophy. It does not matter in what shape we meet it: whether it takes the form of Marxism, or Nazism, or the less militant and more intellectual forms of Logical Positivism and Existentialism, it is always the same creed: the denial of God, the self-sufficiency of Man. They can all be fought with the same weapons which, spiritually speaking, are faith in God and courage. The disciples used no others, and this is a timeless battle which is never modern and never out of date, so the weapons, too, are ageless.

In the case of the first three, Christians are more or less clear as to the position and the tactics of the opposing army, but in the case of Existentialism there seems an occasional tendency to forgather among both leaders and rank and file; to have days of unofficial truce in much the same way as English and German soldiers forgathered on one of the Christmas Days in World War I. It was all very casual and very friendly, but it did not do much to help the fighting of the next morning. Such a tendency must surely have its dangers or Pope Pius XII would not find it necessary, in *Humani Generis*, to warn the world against it.

In the attempt to get some sort of Christian form of Existentialism, the idea, as far as one can gather, appears to be to choose the best points in that philosophy, and try to adapt them to Christianity by giving them a religious turn. This is, perhaps, a non-professional view of the matter, but when all is said and done, very few of us are professional philosophers. Meanwhile, since these best points were Christian long before they were Existentialist—using that word to denote the new mode of thought only—it strikes one as a little superfluous.

Take, for instance, its teaching on the upward trend of the human being. Man is invited to live his life by dint of effort: transcending, moment by moment, his actual state. In each life, we are told, there should be a definite struggle towards personal conversion. Existence is a conquest, according to Jaspers, but a conquest achieved by a rhythm of recurring crisis—of flux and reflux—defeat and victory. "A perpetual storm of antinomies" and an attempt at equilibrium by means of "an effort of painful and never-ending tension".

St. Paul seems to have noticed something of the sort a good many years before Jaspers, and the analogy is perhaps instructive. "For that which I work I understand not. For I do not that good which I will; but the evil which I hate, that I do. . . . For I am delighted with the law of God, according to the inward man; but I see another law in my members, fighting against the law of my mind and captivating me in the law of sin that is in my members. Unhappy man that I am. . . ."

According to Gabriel Marcel also, our motto should not be *sum* but *sursum*. Man must act—dare—play his hand in the game of life. He should not live from day to day, careless of his destiny; but, being free, he is bound to use his gift of choice continually; he must give himself, engage himself, in relation to his own destiny and that of others.

This is all no doubt very forceful and very delightful,

particularly to enquiring youth, but is it so very *new*, after all? Was it not all said to us two thousand years ago, and very much better said? "Master, what must I do to inherit eternal life? Jesus asked him, What is it that is written in the law? What is thy reading of it? And he answered, Thou shalt love the Lord thy God with the love of thy whole heart, and thy whole soul, and thy whole strength, and thy whole mind; and thy neighbour as thyself. Thou hast answered right, He told him; do this and thou shalt find life."

Man must love with the love of his whole heart, his whole soul, his whole strength and his whole mind, first God, then his neighbour. Man must give himself, engage himself, in relation to his own destiny and that of others. What are the words of Marcel but a faint echo of the words of Christ? Why not take them therefore direct from Christ instead of claiming them for Existentialism? Why not practise Christianity itself, *tout court*? It will cover the whole of theist Existentialism, that is certain— and a good deal more that has been left out.

If Existentialism were an universal doctrine: if it dealt with the State, the masses, with general propositions, it might be argued that all these had changed with a changing world and required new treatment. But, on the contrary, it is specifically claimed that the philosophy is entirely subjective, human, personal; and we are all agreed, surely, that Man himself does not change much with the ages?

Solomon was a good deal wiser than most of the world's leaders to-day, and he appears to have faced much the same problems, psychologically speaking, as the Existentialists. To the practical mind it does seem a little unnecessary to confuse other people's beliefs with a theist version of a philosophy the main point of which is atheism. There is at least this to be said for the logic of the pagan Existentialists: they have not, so far, launched an atheist version of Christianity.

This is a fight of the whole world, and it is a bigger affair than the quarrels of rival philosophies. It is the old fundamental quarrel between God and the devil—Lucifer and Michael. Whether it hides behind the figures of Marx, or Hitler, or Sartre, that is always the real issue, and not the political and psychological jargon which cloaks it. While one type of Existentialism may advertise itself as Christian, there is surely no need for Christianity to advertise itself as Existentialist? After all, one does not drop the sea into a river: one drops the river into the sea.

Choice — freedom — commitment — giving ourselves whole-heartedly to life—these are the catchwords of modern psychology which attract. Just as there is a good side to such teaching in its opposition to Totalitarianism, so also it does undoubtedly try to force its followers to think, to decide, to choose. It has no use for the person who drifts. But, once more, why claim that this is either new or exclusive? Robert Browning was writing his poems a hundred years ago, and this is the end of one of them, as we all know. It is as frankly pagan and misguided in its sentiments as any of theirs.

> " The true has no value beyond the sham:
>   As well the counter as coin, I submit,
>   When your table's a hat, and your prize, a dram,
>
> Stake your counter as boldly every whit,
>   Venture as warily, use the same skill,
>   Do your best, whether winning or losing it,
>
> If you choose to play!—is my principle.
>   Let a man contend to the uttermost
>   For his life's set prize, be it what it will! "

Had Browning lived to-day, the Existentialists would certainly have claimed him; but I am not quite sure that he would have been flattered.

Roger Troisfontaines says that Christianity and Existentialism are not actually opposed upon either their method or their fundamental doctrine: it is the contention of both that each man must freely determine his existence. But let us go back oné step further: *why* does he have to do so? Who gave him that power and obligation? The Christian answers God. What does the Existentialist answer?

This may perhaps be what Wells bitterly called "the feminine mode of argument", but to the unsubtle intellect it does occur that methods are secondary to results: that the manner of approach is less vital than the conclusions which the approach produces. In this particular case the conclusions must obviously be Existential, since it is existence which is being considered. The point then is this: is the kind of life lived by a Marcel, and the kind of life advocated by a Sartre, as a result of their respective philosophies, likely to have anything in common or to end in the same conduct? If not, why call them by the same name? Verbally, at all events, one arrives at suicide and the other at salvation.

As far as one can see, the misery of the atheist Existentialist is chiefly caused by the double consciousness of his freedom in every sense, particularly his freedom of choice, and his despair at the sort of world in which he has to exercise it. His despair is therefore in reality solely due to his atheism. If he believed in God, saw life as part of eternity and the world as God's creation, there would be nothing to be in despair about. This is the position of Marcel who now admits that the two creeds have but little in common.

The danger to the ordinary Christian who becomes

involved mentally in all this sophistry, is that, if parts of the philosophy are represented as being right, and parts as not, how are we to know which to take and which to leave? There was once a lady president of a Shakespeare Club, in the vanished days when ladies were careful as to what they repeated, and in preparing her notes she particularly marked all the passages which had better not be quoted in the lecture which she proposed to give to the society. And then unfortunately on the evening itself she got confused, and read out all the marked passages and left out all the others: a fate which might perhaps overtake us also if we indulged in too much Existentialism.

The pagan Existentialist wishes to be his own God. "Here", says Père Grevillot, "is what Catholic theology calls the sin of Lucifer."[1] To a simple soul it seems clear that one cannot have a Catholic form of the sin of Lucifer—at least not an approved one. One might as well speak of a Catholic form of Marxism, or of Catholic Stoicism or Catholic Hedonism, since Catholic philosophy undoubtedly urges us to practise the three principal characteristics of those other creeds: brotherhood, resignation and joyousness.

We do not need to be Existentialists in name to know that the modern world has gone awry. Modern art, with its one eye where we used to expect two, and its square heads where we had once thought to see them oval, reflects unmistakably the state of mind of the present generation. One naturally does not see quite as far round with one eye, even if it is placed in the middle, as with two, one at each side, such as were common in the old days. And one imagines that the contents of a square head would somehow be different from the contents of a round one. Certain it is, at all events, that a round

_____
[1] *Les Grands Courants de la Pensée Contemporaine*, p. 16.

room is much easier to keep clean than a square one, and does not collect dust to anything like the same ghastly degree. But this again, of course, may be only the feminine method of reasoning.

The clearest thing that emerges at the end of all the discussions and the arguments and the exhortations is that in our period, more perhaps than any other, Christians must be practical. Roger Troisfontaines remarks that above all the religious man of to-day must translate his principles " into the language of the thought of his period ".[2] When one is a Christian, he suggests, is it not obviously just this task, this effort of translation, which constitutes fidelity to Christ?

Père Grevillot says much the same thing.[3] He tells us that many of the deported waifs and strays of Europe have noticed the fact that whereas, in the utter misery to which they were reduced by their circumstances, they were at first tempted to abandon both faith and ideals, after a time, seeing from the living examples around them to what a pitch of selfish degradation this could reduce a human being, they reacted by a sudden rebound of courage, and so saved their human values.

Modern society, he concludes, is inclined to turn away from mere logic, since the deductions of logic are often fallacious, behind their apparently solid exterior. Instead, this generation is thirsty for life itself, since life, it imagines, does not cheat.

"It seems that actual society, obeying a reflex movement of deliverance, is in search of a doctrine which will save it. . . . It is ready to listen to whoever will speak to it of hope in a language which it can understand. . . . We are thus invited and encouraged to action. Existen-

[2] *Existentialisme et Pensée Chrétienne.* Troisfontaines. p. 88.
[3] *Les Grands Courants de la Pensée Contemporaine.* Grevillot. p. 61, etc.

tialist literature is, as it were, the cry of distress of a world which is perishing and calls for help. It shows that this is no moment for theoretical disputes: it is the moment for a creed and a work of salvation. In our day two principal philosophies call man to this effort of rescue and transformation: Marxism and Christianity."

CHAPTER XVIII

THE PSYCHOLOGIST AND THE CONTEMPLATIVE

"OH, dear!" said the novice leaning over Sister Imelda and regarding her with alarm. "Would you like me to fetch someone?"

There was no need, for I was close on her heels and already staring past her at our hermit who, most unaccountably, was lying on her back in the middle of the lavender bed. Apparently she was engaged in contemplating the blue sky above.

"Is anything the matter, Sister? Shall I help you up?"

"By no means," replied Sister Imelda, folding her hands placidly across her front, "that is, if you don't mind? I tripped over a stone and happened to fall backwards into the bushes—I am having such a nice rest—beautiful smell—lovely sky—I was a little tired—delightful. . . ."

Sister Elizabeth and I looked at each other; then we looked at our prostrate desert-dweller; finally we both sat back on our heels, one on each side of her.

"You get quite a different view from your back, don't you?" she remarked conversationally. "Like staring at the ceiling as a child, and thinking how much more interesting it was than the floor, and how nice it would be to walk about on it. The clouds look quite soft from down here, and the sun is coming through. . . ."

"Well, don't go and walk about on them yet please," said I.

"Oh, *no!*" cried Sister Elizabeth.

A hen which had been scratching not far away moved nearer. "Rosalie," murmured Sister Imelda, closing her eyes, "she has not been very well; it is her time for occupational therapy."

"Her time for what?"

"Scratching for insects," explained the novice.

Sister Imelda has lately been making a new rock-garden with the assistance of her neophyte, and a very charming little piece of landscape work it is. We were on the edge of it now. It runs from the cloister-end of the house right down past the kitchen, and there is a special enclosure which, Sister Imelda assures me, is reserved exclusively for myself. She has chosen quite the most salubrious spot for it, I must say, exactly between the windows of the kitchen and the scullery, because it has a little square of flagged cement where I can sit on even the dampest evening, between compline and matins, and read. That is the idea. There is also a nice sink-drain which, as Sister Imelda has pointed out several times with special pride, marks the end of the enclosure, and as she has painted its surround a beautiful white, no one can possibly make a mistake. Beyond that, no other human foot must tread.

"You see, you can either sit with your face to it, so very private; or with your back to it and admire the flowers."

"I quite understand," I said warmly, "the drain is mine." And I sat down with my face to it. It happened to be a Sunday afternoon when she first showed me round my new domain, and then went away leaving me to enjoy the sabbath peace. After a time, a certain restlessness came over me. Did it, or did it not? Was it, or was it not? I tried to believe it did not, and that it was coming from something else: maybe from one of the strange new Eastern plants that she had been given. Anyway, she had assured me more than once that she had put plenty of Izal down it, so I should come to no harm—all the same—was it, or was it not? I turned my back to it to see if that were any better. There were some delightful little tulips and dwarf-peonies at my feet, and after a few minutes I went on with the reading. Over my shoulder there floated an unmistakable whiff: I glued my eyes to the page and proceeded relentlessly, although the holiness of the thoughts expressed failed somehow completely to captivate my mind. I found myself trying to remember what were the first symptoms of typhoid, a painful disease I believe which I have not yet had, and I wished that the Izal powder had been stronger.

"You look simply heavenly sitting there," cried the delighted voice of Sister Imelda, now back from shutting up her fowls, "so at peace, so mediæval, so almost unearthly. . . ."

"Yes, I feel a bit mediæval and unearthly," I admitted, getting up and joining her on the path, "shall we walk along to the other end and see what your beautiful carnations are doing?"

"Carnations?" repeated Sister Imelda. "But they are not out just now, not for several weeks. . . ."

"I know, I know, but I just want to see what they are *doing*—most interesting plants." I led the way and reluctantly she followed, but, as we went, unfortunately we passed the other drain, and it was altogether too much for her. She halted with a beaming smile.

"You know, I have been thinking," she said, "as you like your garden so much, shall we extend it right up to here, and include. . . ."

"No, no, it is perfect as it is, quite perfect; I mustn't be selfish; I could not think of taking *both*, you know. . . ."

"I could easily put a white surround to it, and plenty of Izal powder. . . ."

"You mustn't think of it," I assured her earnestly, "after all, I could not sit beside two drains at once, and not everybody has even one drain to themselves. . . ." I was getting quite feverish about it, and could not remember what it was that bloomed before carnations. Was it stocks? Perhaps it was hollyhocks. I tried them but found that it was not, and that anyway hollyhocks don't grow in a rock-garden.

"Well, show me what does come out next then?" I begged insinuatingly. She immediately led the way back to the scullery window and together we inhaled the sweet scent of Izal on a May afternoon.

I was recalled to the present moment by the voice of Sister Imelda suddenly rising from the ground, with an uncanny effect like the blood of Abel crying to the Lord.

"I think I will get up now," she said, firmly grasping a lavender bush. Sister Elizabeth and I tugged simultaneously from either side, and, after a moment of painful suspense, we all came up together, lavender bush included.

"Put it in again," said Sister Imelda, over her shoulder, as I led her unresisting to the stone parapet which serves also as a garden bench. Sister Elizabeth did so gravely, then followed us, trowel in hand.

"I have had a letter from Monsignor in Rome which I thought might interest you both." I sat down, unfolded it and spread it out, metaphorically put on spectacles and prepared to edify. Sister Imelda slipped her hands under her scapular and stared at me, waiting respectfully for the utterances of Authority. Sister Elizabeth also put her hands under her scapular, trowel and all, and cast her eyes down upon the ground. It was I who was edified.

"He wants to know how you are getting on, Sister, and he says that the greatest difficulty for the modern novice appears to be obedience: that is according to the various novice-masters he has consulted for me."

"Ah!" said Sister Imelda and Sister Elizabeth simultaneously; but they said nothing more so I was not much the wiser.

"He talks a great deal about the Ignatian method of obedience, but I won't read all that, because after three pages he says he does not think it is very suitable for us. That is the way men always get out of things. It was specially noticeable in one of those new books, the ones you used for pressing the Christmas cards. It works down, most methodically, through the whole history and development of religious obedience: the hermits, the cenobites, the old orders of monks and friars and the clerks regular: then it discusses the theology of religious obedience, the doctrine of religious obedience, religious obedience according to Canon Law: and after having brought us successfully all that way, quite suddenly the author puts his finger to his lip and steals away on tiptoe. 'The Mystery of Woman and Religious Obedience', he calls the next chapter, and it is all about the mystery and hardly a word about the obedience."

"The mystery," said Sister Imelda reflectively, "is of course as old as Eve, but it is the mystery of her disobedience and not what he thinks it is. *That's* the trouble."

"Ah!" said Sister Elizabeth and I simultaneously, and we said nothing more. Like the author of the book, I suppose we felt that there was nothing more to be said. We all three stared at each other.

"Shall I read you the rest?"

Anthony, who had been trapeezing like a monkey in the trees overhead for several minutes in a well-meant effort to attract our attention, suddenly made a forced landing without his under-carriage down. "Serves you right for showing off," said Sister Imelda as he picked himself up and joined the party. Thus encouraged I proceeded.

"'The modern spirit is athirst not so much for pleasure as for liberty and independence: it is a reaction against war and post-war conditions: restrictions, rationing: personal independence becomes the only possible refuge and relief. There is undoubtedly a serious problem to be faced in our time which, as a matter of fact, comes to a head in the following painful paradox. The Gospel has, as it were, been re-discovered by this generation: the Gospel with all its stark insistence on the beauty and the necessity of obedience, crowned by the unique example of obedience of God made man—obedience even unto death.

"'And yet, this is the paradox: with it all, Christ Himself was the first and best teacher of true liberty. "The sabbath was made for man, not man for the sabbath." St. Paul, his disciple, coming after him, went even further: "We can do service in a new manner, according to the spirit, not according to the letter as of old."[1] Or again: "There must a turning to the Lord first, and then the veil will be taken away. The spirit we have been speaking of is the Lord; and where the Lord's spirit is, there is freedom. It is given to us, all alike, to catch the glory of the Lord as in a mirror, with faces unveiled; and so we become transfigured into the same likeness, borrowing glory from that glory, as the Spirit of the Lord enables us".'[2]

"That's lovely!" cried Sister Elizabeth spontaneously.

[1] St. Paul's Epistle to the Romans vii, 6.
[2] St. Paul's II Epistle to the Corinthians iii, 17.

"'How to reconcile the two,' he says, 'that is the problem for this generation—and it is what causes trouble in Novitiates.'"

"You know," said Sister Imelda, "the choice put before Adam and Eve was not quite the choice the devil made it seem to them. And the choice which we have now is not quite what he makes it seem to us either. They appear to have imagined that the choice lay between servitude to God—and don't touch the apple—or eat it and, with the eating, receive the knowledge of gods and so full liberty and the end of all servitude. It was the end of all servitude which really attracted them, as it does us still now. That's what they expected. And, of course, it doesn't exist. The real choice only lay between the free and loving service of God, which they then enjoyed with all its unspeakable happiness, and the servitude of sin into which they immediately fell. Poor Adam and Eve: such a shock. The devil was only offering them the choice between God and himself to serve, and that was the long and the short of it. And that is where our choice still lies, only he wraps it up so. Shall we listen to some more?"

"'Although still, as a race, under the yoke of sin, Christ, by His obedience unto death, has given us back our royal liberty and the power to win heaven again by a free and loving worship of God. *Servire Deo regnare est.* What St. Paul calls the "glorious liberty of the children of God". That is the spiritual liberation offered us, if only we know how to accept it, and our great means as Christians of accepting it and increasing it day by day, is the *Truth*. The more we know God, who is Truth itself, the more we come to know ourselves; and the better we know ourselves, the greater becomes our sense of personal freedom.'"

Sister Elizabeth looked doubtful. "The better I get

to know myself the more of a fool I feel," she remarked candidly. I hurried on.

"'A novice-master drew my attention the other day, while we were walking on the Albanian hills—ask your novice if she remembers the hills around Albano'— There!" I stopped abruptly. "Isn't that just like a man to go and put in a hopeless question of that sort so unexpectedly that I hadn't time to switch off and stop its coming out. How was I to know that he was going to talk about sunsets and things right in the middle of a theological discourse?"

"Anyway you missed out the sunset," said Sister Imelda soothingly.

"Yes, I did—at least nearly," I replied shortly. Sister Elizabeth looked pensive—but eminently holy and re-signed.

"Well, anyway, 'A novice-master drew my attention to'—um—yes——" I turned the pages hastily, and, thank God, came to theology again, "' to a most interest-ing fact. Obedience teaches us to act, not by childish caprice, not even for reasonable and virtuous reasons, but *for the common good*. That is the rectifying quality which lies behind all its training, and which he always stresses to his novices.'"

"The last bit was only a stage-direction," remarked Sister Imelda, "you should not have included it in the discourse. She'll know what you are doing next time."

"Well, it's a good thing somebody should know," I suggested practically, "do you want me to finish or do you not?"

"Oh, please!" they cried together. I took it that they meant not to finish, so I went on.

"' It teaches us not to act for selfish, personal motives, but to act for the *best* and from motives of charity. The

M

judgment, so far from being set on one side, learns to appreciate the difference between the welfare of one and the welfare of many. The sense of responsibility thus develops, because a real responsibility is felt towards all.'"

"I thought you said it was an interesting fact," observed Sister Imelda in a slightly depressed voice.

"It is," I reassured her, "we're just coming to the interest: that was only the fact. 'After years of willing service of God, offered through the channel of obedience, in any sudden, unforeseen situation, where immediate action is called for, the religious concerned will afterwards be found to have done, in the absence of any order or command whatsoever, absolutely the correct thing, and what would have been judged right had there been time to express a wish. The *spirit* has absorbed the long teaching of years, the main principles to be acted upon—charity, humility, truth, courtesy—and there is no longer need for the swaddling-clothes of spiritual infancy.'" I stopped.

"Well, I suppose you could not remain an idiot all your life," said Sister Imelda hopefully, "unless, of course, you really were."

"Oh, dear," murmured Sister Elizabeth with a sigh, "I am sure I ought to feel better, but somehow I don't."

"You are an impossible audience. Impossible. I shall not read you any more. Here have I been at it for nearly twenty minutes, and it has come all the way direct from Rome, and you are not a bit uplifted. Not a bit." I looked at Sister Imelda. She smiled her slow smile and glanced at the novice.

"Do you want it put into everyday language?" she asked kindly.

"I want something that will help me to *do* it, not to talk about it."

"Well, then, listen: the woman speaks. Only the woman: Eve over again. She can't compete with male theory, but *Eve knows*. She knows because she started it all, ages back, and she hasn't altered fundamentally since then. The mystery is not much mystery to her. The new Eve is redeemed now, of course, but the old Eve knew something else; something that we can never know. She knew what it was to be absolutely perfect— before she sinned. If we have our contrasts to-day, she had worse contrasts. Poor Eve."

"Poor us," said the novice.

"No, happy us. All these modern, so-called psychological problems melt into thin air when we learn to love. We religious are the specialists in obedience—we have to offer that to God in atonement for the recalcitration of the world—but it has nothing to do with this absurd fog of psychiatry. The whole matter is spiritual, not psychological. We religious give our obedience, purely and simply, to the will of God. The first step towards doing the will of God is, after all, to stop doing our own. That is all that the religious is aiming at in taking a vow of obedience to a superior. The old religious gets to the point where she identifies herself wholly with the will of God purely by means of the will of the superior, which is no more to her than the sure manifestation of God's will for her personally. The wise religious learns to hold all things so lightly that God can take, and replace, them at will. But that does not mean not caring. *Never that.* The person who simply learnt not to care, to become selfish and callous, could never love the will of God with a burning love, and that is how it has to be loved in religion." She turned to the novice. "You *do* love God's will like that, don't you?"

Sister Elizabeth is utterly honest; I will say that much

180180

for her. She blushed but she looked Sister Imelda straight in the face.

"Theoretically I do," she replied, "but when it comes to the point, I am afraid I often find myself hoping that His will will manage to coincide with mine."

"But even when it doesn't, you do it," said Sister Imelda gently, "and the other will pass. You know how it is in ordinary life. If we love any person very much we honestly want them to have their way rather than that we should have ours. That is one of the greatest gifts of love, to give us the power to rejoice more in the pleasure and happiness of another than in our own. The strongest passion always wins in the end, and our strongest passion must be that God should rule everywhere, in that perfect harmony which existed at the beginning of the world when everything was just as He intended." She looked at Sister Elizabeth again and smiled.

"Love, that is all. How? Why, with the same process by which we love ordinary people. We don't make ourselves love them, do we? It is they who make us. Sheer attraction. But we have to allow ourselves to feel it. Sometimes the attraction is so strong that they can even make us love them when we would rather not. That, although you do not realize it, is the stage you have reached with God." The novice gave a little start and opened her eyes wide. Sister Imelda nodded in the friendliest fashion.

"Yes, you are still inclined to struggle and fight over it. I expect, you know, that you want to keep a lot of things for yourself, and you realize subconsciously that you can't do that if you love." She got up slowly. "Don't worry about yourself and how you feel. Turn round instead and ask God to go on making you love Him— until you love him *to distraction*. A saint said that, didn't she, and it seems to have succeeded not only for earth but for heaven. Try it."

She moved away, I folded up the letter and put it back in its envelope. Anthony rolled over on his back, purring. " Well! " said Sister Elizabeth.

CHAPTER XIX

EXISTENTIALISM AND ETERNAL
EXISTENCE

I N the parlour the other day one of the younger generation was talking to me about life in general. She
held forth with that delightful candour which is one
of the characteristics of the modern young woman. I
was inclined to commiserate with her on present conditions, but she was cheerfully undaunted. She was conscious of them but not particularly dismayed.

"What you have not had," she insisted gaily, "you do
not miss. We have never had security. For us war, or
at least the likelihood of it, is normal. Normal things
don't get on your nerves in the same way. It's you older
ones," she added generously, "for whom I feel so sorry.
You haven't been trained to stand up to this sort of
thing." I stood up to that anyway.

Recently I heard a dry but excellent definition of the
modern optimist: "a person who still believes in the
uncertainty of the future". The jibe is perhaps well
deserved; too many of us have drifted over to the habitually gloomy view. We forget, maybe, that although
truth should never be considered as relative, our values
may often be comparative: that is to say, they will depend to a certain extent upon what we already have and
what we may therefore reasonably expect to get.

"They have everything they want," is an expression
one frequently hears, yet after all it covers widely different standards. In one case it may mean a large country
house and the latest touring-car and in another a semi-

detached villa with three bedrooms and a new bicycle. The proud possessors are equally satisfied and happy.

It is exactly the same for our spiritual values. The values of a saint are so simple, and so concentrated, that there is almost no comparison possible between them and those of the ordinary good Christian. It is no longer a question of a villa and a mansion, it is a question of holding a farthing candle to the sun, or balancing earth and heaven. The values of a saint, one imagines, must be almost completely pure values. God is his sole end, and God his sole means. Meanwhile the mixture of dross and gold which serves for the rest of us would be appalling were it not so pathetic. Half the time we scarcely seem to distinguish the difference, and offer God the one for the other with almost incredible complacency.

As the Existentialists tell us, man is "a creature of distances," and so our values are a curious mixture of past, present and future, and of subconscious comparisons which we can hardly explain even to ourselves. That is one of the things which make the modern pagan philosophies so insidious. They deal largely with the future, and draw a subtly derogatory picture of the past and the present. Any philosophy to succeed to-day must point the way to a sunny to-morrow, as Marxism does, and as Existentialism tries to do—and so singularly fails.

"Man is the future of Man", is one of its mottoes. He makes his own future, and he makes it unaided. He is a hero if he makes himself a hero: he is a coward only if he makes himself a coward. Such teaching is dangerous because it is such a treacherous mixture of truth and falsehood, and because, in spite of its falsity, it does undoubtedly seem to provide an answer to the subconscious aspirations of youth. In our young and golden days it is a great thing to feel that we are the masters of our fate; that the untried future which lies before us can be moulded to our desires and to the secret ambitions of our hearts. And, of course, *under God*, it is all so true. But *under God*.

In Him we are indeed the masters of our circumstances: we can modify them: we can ennoble them: if we let Him go for a moment we can inexpressibly degrade them. Nevertheless the fact remains that we did not make them in the beginning, neither can we completely and finally bring them to an end. The Existentialist, of course, claims that we can. In the last resort we can end ourselves—as our final and unanswerable demonstration of personal liberty. It takes a Christian to know that that mad act ends nothing. It only takes us to another and eternal set of circumstances, equally created by God. For hell was made by God—and the devil only went there. He went there of his own free will, and we can go with him if we wish. That is our liberty. We can choose God or the devil for eternity: but choose one or the other we must.

We who have deliberately chosen God, know that we are at least on the right side of this ideological world-war of to-day, but our difficulty, as ordinary rank and file, is to know just how to fight for our religion and our beliefs by words or by argument. The answer, in at least five cases out of ten, is 'don't'. For the theologian it is, of course, a much more simple matter, although not even for the theologian is every moment a suitable moment in which to argue theology.

The Marxist and the Existentialist hold us here at a distinct disadvantage. For them, the world is their play-ground—and their battlefield. Their philosophies are material, sensational, emotional: aimed at the world and designed for the world. They can preach them in season and out of season, and so long as they do not attempt to preach them in church, the setting is probably not too inappropriate. But the Christian is on quite a different footing. There are many occasions, and many places, unavoidable for people living in the world, in which openly to preach his religion would be to do more harm than good.

That was one of the difficulties of my young friend in the parlour. "All this Catholic Action business," she called it disrespectfully. I pointed out to her the error of her ways.

"It's all very well for you to talk, you don't have to do it," she grumbled.

"I didn't know you did," I suggested mildly.

"Well, unofficially I've tried it, and with me, frankly, it just doesn't work. I was half thinking of offering myself for one of those Secular-Institute things, and I thought I'd see how I got on at it first. I didn't get on."

"What happened?"

"I started off one day at the office. That's supposed to be the right place. Said my 'Hail Mary' to myself and everything too. First they laughed and then they got bored. I didn't mind their laughing, but when they got bored I said: 'This is no life for me'."

"But what did you *do*?—— To bore them I mean?"

She wriggled uncomfortably. "Oh, well, I just talked you know. About religion, and going to church, and all that, and being good, and helping our mothers at home."

"Camilla, you little idiot! No wonder they laughed."

"I do help her—sometimes that is—really I do," said Camilla blushing. "But when I got on to church it was worse."

I was not surprised to hear it. "What did you say about *that*?" I enquired apprehensively.

"I said that it was our absolute duty to go, whether we liked it or not, and that after all, as we didn't go for anything but Our Lord, the preacher, and all that, didn't matter one way or the other."

"Help! " I ejaculated faintly. "Camilla, my child, what you want is a muzzle and not a Secular Institute; drop that idea out of your mind."

Her case, I suspect, is the case of many. Are they then to remain entirely silent, to treat their religion as though it were not a part of everyday life? The answer may be that actions speak louder than words, and that there is no company in which they cannot behave as Christians, no occasion upon which they cannot unobtrusively act their belief.

That is one of the few tactical points upon which we are in a better position than our opponents. Were they to drop propaganda and take instead to direct action, the results would probably be disastrous even from their point of view; but the acts of a Christian, if consistent with his Faith, can never, under any circumstances, be that. On the contrary, they will often translate for him, into a mute but comprehensible language, beliefs which on many occasions he could not suitably put into words.

What did Our Lord do when on earth? Whenever He found Himself among those who had followed Him to listen, who were waiting to be taught, eager for His preaching, He gave them what they asked. But when He found Himself in the company of those who were either too hard of heart, or too proud of intellect, or too ignorant as yet to grasp His teaching, instead He took to acts—which for Him were miracles. He healed the sick, He raised the dead, He fed the hungry, He *showed* them what they would only have scoffed at had He tried to say it. If we are His disciples, what better way can we take than His own?

It is extraordinary what a profound effect we can have on others, and indeed this effect is something from which we cannot escape. No one can be so hidden, so apparently isolated, as not to affect someone. Human solidarity is a very real thing: Père Grevillot points out that we are not always sufficiently aware of the bearing of our words and our actions, which to us seem so insignificant. Our personal responsibility for the effect which we produce, and must produce whether we will or no, is very great if only we realized it—and this, however unimportant we may happen to be.[1]

If we wish to judge adequately of our effect upon others, let us consider the effect of others upon ourselves. We may think that we are not much influenced by those around us but on reflection we shall find that unconsciously we are. The Existentialists have, in fact, drawn attention to some interesting psychological tendencies in this connection. One of them uses this very simple illustration: he supposes that he has so far forgotten himself as to stop in a passage and look through a keyhole. Somebody passes by and sees him. Immediately he becomes aware of the extreme vulgarity of his action and is ashamed.

From this he draws the conclusion that other men are necessary to him in order, as it were, to show him to himself: to make him realize what manner of man he is. In his contacts with them he learns to know his own faults, his own tendencies and feelings. It would seem that he regards other men in something of the light in which we Christians regard our conscience. He makes them the arbiters of his conduct, and of what he may and may not do—after which he complains, rather unreasonably under the circumstances, that they curtail his liberty.

He also appears a little piqued that they do not sufficiently consider his dignity. Whereas to himself he is

[1] *Les Grands Courants de la Pensée Contemporaine.* Grevillot. p. 29.

the subject of all his thrilling experiences, to others, much to his disgust, he finds that he is only an object. He draws the comparison between himself and an ink-pot: to another man, he complains, he is merely something sitting upon a chair, just as the inkpot is something sitting upon the table. Even when he is looking through his keyhole he regrets that he is no more to the passer-by than "an object leaning over it as a tree might be inclined by the wind". Personally, if I were engaged in looking through a keyhole, I should be very grateful to mean no more than that to anyone who happened to see me, but we must allow for the peculiar temperament of the Existentialist.

Such reflections, however, make one wonder whether some of the involuntarily dislike, or shall we call it lack of appreciation, which we occasionally feel towards other people, and for which in private we beat our breasts, may not be merely what one might call an objective dislike caused by purely exterior circumstances? To go back to the illustration of the inkpot on the table: if every time I put out my hand to pick up something else, I knock over the inkpot, in the end I get annoyed with it, however nice an inkpot it may be in itself.

It might perhaps be worth our while to consider some of our more unreasonable antipathies in this light, and to notice whether they may not be caused merely by the fact that the people in question are an obstacle to some desired end or plan of our own. Were we to meet them under other circumstances, we might find them quite congenial, or were we to change our own objective, we might then discover that they no longer worried us.

For us the practical upshot of all these introspective heart-searchings is to make us realize that, while the Christian takes the commandments of God as his rule of conduct and thus sets himself a supernatural standard to which to attain, our Existentialist sets himself only the purely human standard of what other men will think of him: a standard which, apart from everything else, is so variable as to have no intrinsic value whatsoever. After all, among cannibals it is considered quite the thing to eat the stranger who happens, unfortunately for himself, to cross one's path.

There can be no real hope, and therefore no real happiness, except in God. That is the simple truth to which we always come back. Indeed, even the " theist-Existentialist ", who is trying to make a compromise between his theories and the existence of God, has to rely on that as his foundation. The others, the atheists, say frankly that, in the end, their conclusions only bring them to a sensation of nausea, of futility and despair: which is, could they but see it, a tacit acknowledgment of the existence of God, without whom they can find nothing worth while on earth.

To get at the real meaning of life we have to return to the Gospels, to see what Man's liberty meant to Christ Himself. That is the only view of it which matters in the end. It meant the liberty then, as it still does, to reject Him. It meant the liberty then, as it still does, to choose Him and to win heaven. He respected the liberty of each individual whom He met. His disciples, when they were called, were free to follow Him or not, and so they remain to-day. To Matthew he said ' Come ', and to the rich young man the same. One came, the other turned away, just as we see it happening in our own time; but precisely what that coming or turning away means, we can never assess in this life. We must wait to know.

Meanwhile happiness, peace, joy, remain the real tests of the soundness of our beliefs: but it is the happiness and the peace of Christ Himself on earth, and of the

Saints who have followed after Him, and it does not exclude suffering. It is a happiness which, for us, rests upon supernatural hope. "Happiness is a feeling peculiar to the individual, which means for him, realization of his destiny," writes Père Grevillot. "It is not just a feeling of pleasure or of power, but consciousness of a perfection of our Being which gives us an eternal value."

This is the sort of philosophy with which we have to defeat the new pagan philosophies, but it is philosophy which, even more than theirs, has to be lived in order to have its full effect. True, they may think theirs out to a conclusion which at all events satisfies them but, in spite of all their protests, they do not live them to any conclusion at all. For our part, if we do not live our religion worthily in practice, it will be of very little use either to ourselves or to anyone else. What there was to be said about it, was said in essence two thousand years ago, and it will never be said more truly or more attractively. It can be amplified, but amplification does not change fundamental truth. Meanwhile, the need and the duty to live it will continue so long as the world lasts.

Other philosophies have their day and their vogue and fade away; they become only an interesting matter of history; they are spoken of mainly in the past and as having once swayed the minds and the conduct of men. But this great philosophy of Christ, this amazing way of life, which is able to teach us not only how to live happily now, but how to live eternally in unclouded joy, is something above and beyond all the ephemeral thoughts of Man. Existentialists all, but ours is a way of eternal existence. Clear—so clear before us that a child cannot miss it—yet so profound that the wisest man on earth would find life too short to fathom it.

Let them read their volumes of fashionable philosophy; let them study the situations they find in them, and be amused and intrigued by the artificial dialogues. To-day no doubt those books may be seen on the tables of every society drawing-room, or in paper editions on the factory benches; to-morrow they will be lost and forgotten at the back of dusty shelves. But Christian philosophy has stood the test of the unfolding of two thousand years of human history. And still it is as matchless and as appropriate as on the day when it was first outlined to a wondering generation by Christ Himself. Still it captures its disciples and calls them to leave all and follow, as they left all and followed then. "Though heaven and earth should pass away, my words will stand."

CHAPTER XX

IN THE DAYS OF PINK PLASTIC

THE wide south-west windows of the convent look out over the orchard beyond. It was a golden mid-summer day as through an enchanting network of green and crimson I watched for Sister Imelda. I wanted to talk to her about the swedes. The orange-red crabs were just at their best, as they are with us in July, and the glow of the copper beeches behind, their branches hanging down over the low stone wall, was repeated in the scarlet combs of the scattered Leghorns on the lawn. Some early Michaelmas daisies, pale against the warmth of the old courtyard, seemed to fling a delicate veil of mauve over the bushes beyond.

There are days when the sunshine seems something tangible, as though one could gather it up in handfuls, letting it run through one's fingers again to fall to earth in golden grains. A pleasant enough scene, and at that moment a still pleasanter figure came slowly into sight, trundling a wheelbarrow and followed by Sister Elizabeth carrying a sack flung over her shoulders, and a heavy spade. They were surely going to take up the first main-crop potatoes; this was obviously the moment for swedes.

"Turnips?" said Sister Imelda when I had arrived and explained my business. "You like the yellow ones this year? Very well." She put down her tools but she did not look altogether happy. Neither did Anthony, who was riding majestically, with his most Pekin-Palace expression, in the wheelbarrow, instead of curvetting as usual at her side.

"Anthony is upset altogether—I have hurt his feelings," she said in a melancholy tone. Anthony continued to gaze beyond her with the distant air of an hereditary monarch. "I had to bring him in the wheelbarrow or he would not have come at all."

"Dear, dear!" said I. He turned his head and regarded me listlessly from the state coach.

"I pulled out one of his whiskers—I pulled it hard. It was sticking straight out and all shiny in the sun, and I thought it was a needle which I had lost, so of course I tried to get it back. I have told him that it was a most regrettable mistake but he is mortally offended."

"Anthony," said I, "mice! They are going to dig. Forget your whiskers in the pleasures of sport." I tipped the wheelbarrow sideways and he fell out reluctantly. He still did not look at Sister Imelda, who picked up the spade with a depressed expression. "I would not have hurt his feelings for the world," she said several times; Anthony shivered with pleasure all down his spine but remained stone deaf.

"He'll get over it," I assured her. "Who is going to do the actual digging? I expect Sister Elizabeth wishes we had one of those machines for dealing with this sort of thing?"

She turned quickly. "Oh, no!" she cried. I was surprised, even perhaps a little touched, at the warmth in her voice. "*I* don't want anything changed in Carmel."

Sister Imelda revived somewhat; she regarded her with a twinkling blue eye. "Pray don't include yourself in that remark," she said dryly.

"Oh, no!" cried the novice again, with unabated fervour.

"That is the right idea," I observed approvingly, "our

N

surroundings stand still while we move on. It is so much less confusing than standing still amid a welter of moving objects." Sister Elizabeth put down her sack abruptly; she had forgotten all about potatoes.

"Oh, do explain that," she explained in a relieved tone. "It has been really worrying me. I love it all so much," her voice was shy, "and yet—those books—they seem to suggest—you see, I can't imagine what it would be *like* if it were all up to date!"

"Who said it was going to be all up to date?" enquired Sister Imelda almost sharply. She forgot Anthony.

"Pray discourse to your novice upon the matter which she has raised," said I grandly, waving my hand and sitting down, with rather less pomp, upon the edge of the wheelbarrow. On occasions such as these the novice is her novice, in the same way in which the chickens are occasionally exclusively her chickens. There was absolutely nothing else to sit upon except the ground, but I did not feel that this was a position from which I could fittingly deliver a sermon. "You can balance on the other side, if you will do so in a religious spirit," I said kindly, "but don't get up suddenly, will you?" I know Sister Imelda too well to share a wheelbarrow with her without inserting secret clauses in the agreement. She accepted graciously, while I reflected that the extreme wobbliness of the arrangement would make it easy to bring it to an end at any moment should it be desirable.

"The fact is, the balance of the whole affair is extremely delicate," began Sister Imelda sententiously. "I do not refer to this wheelbarrow alone but to the life of Carmel of which it is perhaps symbolic. It is of old-fashioned construction; I doubt if modern wheelbarrows wobble to this extent."

"They don't," said the novice candidly, "they have contrivances which prevent them."

"Like the modern congregations," replied Sister Imelda. "Well, we haven't. The only thing which keeps us steady is the grace of God. When we don't apply it properly, we don't keep steady, and that is all there is to be said about it."

I felt bound to agree with her. The truth is that in one way we appear to drift further from the world each day, and the world from us, just at the moment when we are called upon to keep in touch with it as never before. Each is caught into a separate stream, set for a different shore. When we reach our haven at last, it will be to be washed up on the miracle of its golden sands by a tide which never ebbs. But the world's restless tide sweeps endlessly backwards and forwards, between the set boundaries of its earthly shores, answering to a strange and wayward attraction, as though drawn and controlled by some fabulous moon of man's own making.

"You see," said Sister Imelda judiciously, "if we were to get too like the world, then what would be the point of leaving it? If we could be us in the world, then why not stay there? But if our life here is such that it could not be lived in the world, then that in itself is our reason for remaining."

"I see," said the novice gravely.

"No, you don't," I assured her with equal gravity, "because that argument is also applicable to an asylum. The life the lunatics lead is such that it could not be led in the world, and that is their reason for remaining where they are. But it does not prove that they are better mad than sane all the same."

This effectually roused our gentle hermit: Anthony might never have existed for all she remembered about his hurt feelings. The wheelbarrow swayed and I was obliged hastily to press my two feet upon the ground to keep us upright. In the interests of psychology I clung on.

" If God has allowed them to be mad, then the poor dears have to stay in a lunatic asylum, and if God has allowed us to be enclosed contemplatives then we have to stay in a convent, but that does not prove that we are lunatics to be in Carmel any more than it proves that they are contemplatives to be in an asylum."

A holy silence brooded over the summer afternoon as we grappled individually with the problem. After some moments I found myself completely stranded with one consideration only: was I mad or was I sane? Which was not, I felt sure, at all what I had meant to consider when I started. How exactly then *had* I started?

" Do you think we could get back to the beginning? " said a small weary voice. " I've got muddled."

" Me too," said Sister Elizabeth.

" Well, the beginning is our vocation, and as we are all sure about that, let's drop the lunatics firmly out of it. As long as we have really got the vocation, and know that we have, it does not matter at all whether . . ."

" Hush—sh—sh——"

" Not at all. I was only going to say that it is not the vocation which we are concerned with at the moment; we have taken that for granted long ago, just as the Holy Father has taken it for granted in *Sponsa Christi*. By the way, have you ever noticed the difference between the two parts of that explanation? The first is telling the world in general *why*; but the rest is only telling us exactly *how*. When it comes to us, ourselves, it is only the setting which is in question; we already know why. The old accusation of the folly of the Cross will always remain at the back of religious life, and has been there ever since the first hermit took his deliberate way to the desert, and the first martyr knew that he was facing death."

"They said Our Lord Himself was mad and had a devil. . . ."

"Granted that we are sane it is really very simple. . . ."

"But I am quite sure that I am sane," remarked Sister Elizabeth plaintively, "I honestly am. There is no need to keep on telling me so; I am not nervous." Sister Imelda laughed. Anthony looked more hurt than ever. How people could be so heartless as to laugh after doing their best to pull other people's whiskers out, was beyond him.

"What even Catholics don't always realize is that the vocation and the setting are inseparable in practice, although not in argument. It comes to this: could we keep the spirit of this vocation in a completely modern atmosphere? For myself, I don't see how. One cannot express the spirit of the great St. Teresa in slacks and Woolworth crockery, because that is not how she expressed it. One might as well tell Turner, now, after his death, to have done his paintings in black and white.

"The contention is that it is no longer genuine poverty to have voluminous habits and old-fashioned brown ware when modern fashions in both would be so much cheaper. We are told that we are paying large sums in order to surround ourselves with an artificial atmosphere which simply annoys postulants who come in having seen real poverty in the world."

"I don't think," said Sister Imelda dryly, "that not to annoy postulants was St. Teresa's first consideration in founding her Reform. Holy Poverty is terribly important, but as a matter of fact it does not come into this affair at all. That is where they go wrong. One might equally say that it is not economical to spend four or five hours a day in going to Mass and reciting the Divine

Office. It isn't. But that has nothing to do with it. We recite the Divine Office for other motives than economy, and it is not brown pottery and yards of thick material which we are paying for, but tradition; and that is always beyond price, as those who have not got it have so frequently found."

Sister Elizabeth nodded.

"I know they say," went on Sister Imelda, "that the dress and all the things used by St. Teresa were in common use in her time (which is also true in the case of all the old Orders) and so we should have things which are in common use now. But what they forget is that the life which St. Teresa followed was also to a large extent in tune with her period, as was that of all the old Orders; or not so different, in any case, as to be completely out of harmony. It was all of a piece. Nothing she used clashed with the inside of a cloister, we may be sure, or she would not have used it. But our life is not in the least in tune with the world of to-day."

I reflected that there was a great deal of truth in what she said. The pictures of that time were full of devotion, and nearly all the great painters chose religious subjects. The furniture might be uncomfortable but it was of beautiful workmanship; all the arts flourished during the Middle Ages and on into the Renaissance. It is true that the year 1576 marked a certain decline in the greatness of Spain, but that would not have affected Teresa, who was by then nearing the end of her own life and work. Michelangelo, Raphael, Leonardo da Vinci, Holbein, Andrea del Sarto, those were the names to conjure with. If this were the common taste of their successive generations, then the common taste might well fit in with a contemplative life. Sister Imelda had evidently been reflecting too, for she raised her head suddenly and stared at me.

"Could *you* lead this life attired in slacks and eating off pink plastic plates?" she demanded. "That is the common taste of *our* day."

Sister Elizabeth and I regarded her in silence.

"You're saints if you could," she said decisively, "I couldn't." It was noticeable that we neither of us offered to be saints.

"The next thing we should have would be the Wireless, and after that, I suppose, Television. Do *they* go with the contemplation of God? Not traditionally certainly. Silence and solitude. The silence of the Wireless and the solitude of a perpetual telescope on to the world. No, if we are going to modernize the old Orders, do not let us trouble to modernize them at all, but declare boldly that they are outworn, and in their place found modern congregations, or else rely entirely upon our Secular Institutes." Sister Elizabeth laughed, but Sister Imelda was quite serious.

I wondered just exactly what the laugh meant. Certainly outwornness was not the note which Pope Pius XII had struck in *Sponsa Christi*, which was, after all, designed to meet modern needs. On the contrary, he reaffirmed the usefulness of the contemplative life, lived as it is lived to-day, and the only modifications which he proposed were those designed to meet specific difficulties arising out of changed social conditions. Work, for instance. He suggested that, if hunger drove as it does some of the Orders abroad, we had better set to, and find some work to do. No one will quarrel with that. It is quite another thing to modernize just for the sake of modernizing; in order to come up to date with a frivolous and pagan world.

"You look very serious, Sister, what are you thinking about?" The novice raised her eyes and dropped them again in that slightly disconcerting way of hers.

"I was thinking of the Queen," she said. "The two Elizabeths—and how different they are. Four hundred years between them; about the same as between St. Teresa and ourselves. But it is not time which separates them; it is the Elizabeths who are so different, they themselves. That is how the changes have come."

And that, of course, is the right way. Changes, in order to be genuine, unaffected changes, should come through changes in people; they should never be imposed from outside. People have to *see* things differently, and change because of a new point of view. Such alterations will always be necessary and will nearly always be improvements; they are made imperceptibly to meet real needs and grow with the years. Looking back, no one can quite remember how they began; they were put into practice bit by bit and without self-consciousness. So the life of enclosed contemplatives has grown out of the past; so it will grow on quietly, imperceptibly, into the future. Not until we are different in spirit from Teresa will the other differences begin. Please God, they are still far distant.

Sister Imelda got up suddenly after all, in spite of the secret clauses to the contrary, and the barrow tipped heavily in my direction.

"Now we are going to take up those potatoes," she said decisively. Anthony hesitated; he knows the word potatoes quite well and to him it expresses those most exciting things, field-mice. He looked at her with his little boot-button eyes to see if she were really sorry. Then he rubbed himself against her habit. After all, she had brought him down in the wheelbarrow.

"The latest machine," said Sister Elizabeth thoughtfully, picking up the spade, "rings a bell every time it drops a seed-potato into the hole it has made; and in the autumn, when it takes them up again, it washes the soil off them, dries them and puts them into a bag. When the bag is full it rings a bell."

"You ought to teach Anthony to be the bell," I said.

"Let us begin," said Sister Imelda, taking no notice whatsoever of my suggestion; "I will dig this end while you pick up the potatoes and put them into the sack. No, Anthony, you need not scratch; if there are any, they will come out of themselves when I dig."

She drove in the spade and up came the potatoes. Sister Elizabeth shook the dry soil from them and dropped them one by one into the empty bag.

"Miaow!" said I over my shoulder, and fled.

CHAPTER XXI

YES OR NO?

ALL that Christ Himself had to say about Christianity, He said two thousand years ago. That is when the Christian philosophy began, but it is not ended yet and never will be. If we take a philosophy such as that of Plato, of Aristotle, of Descartes or Hegel, or of anyone else whom we please, where it ends it ends. Anything added on to it after the death of the great man concerned, is not his philosophy but that of another. But Christ has left behind Him a living and infallible post-explanation of His teaching—His Bride the Church.

L'Abbé Henry Duméry has written a striking passage about this. One thing alone, after all, he says, decides the merits of the Church: that is its Source. In every period it is a question of re-discovering it, perpetually springing forth afresh, perpetually inspiring. It is much better to get back to the fervour of the primitive Church than to have recourse to the so-called 'technique' of to-morrow and the day after. For, from its very beginning, the Church was already complete in the germ, and in full possession of the final aims of its mission. Throughout history it is the same Church which progressively performs the same task. The world may transform itself as much as it likes, but the spirit of the Church, which it awaits and receives, remains unchanged. One might even say that it is this constant variation which demands this indefectible permanence.

He goes on to point out that in this way the oldest

things may after all end by appearing the newest. Fascinated by all our contemporary socialization, we have been working to produce mass-movements, without realizing the almost inevitable chaos which must result from such a method, depending as it does sometimes upon the spiritual, sometimes upon the material, quite indiscriminately. Latterly, however, the world has seen new apostles enter the field: apostles advocating the formation of little islands of Christianity after much the same pattern as those of the primitive apostolic communities. Such was the ideal of Père Godin, of the Mission de France.

In this way we find the twentieth century rejoining the first century of Christianity, so true it is that the apostolate of the Church remains as real and as practical to-day, in a world already grown old, as it was on the threshold of the evangelical era. "And indeed," he adds, "from one end of the history of the Church to the other, there cannot be two ways of making Christians: the conjunction of grace and freewill is always an unique experience which takes place in the depths of the conscience."[1]

L'Abbé Grevillot similarly points out that what are required nowadays above all are courageous men and women. He suggests that there has already been too much compromise. G. Marcel says much the same thing: courage is the distinguishing virtue of the individual, whereas the vague expressions 'they' and 'one' are the breeding-ground of cowardice and evasion. Nothing is more characteristic of the person who sits on the fence than the intellectual subterfuge which takes refuge behind such phrases as . . . 'they maintain' . . . 'one is told that'. . . . The person who uses this sort of language has not even the courage to identify himself with the

[1] *Les Trois Tentations de l'Apostolat Moderne.* Duméry. p. 159.

vague 'they' or 'one' whom he quotes: he literally hides himself behind them.

In spite of the multiple difficulties of our period, the new apostles are all agreed that a healthy optimism is the only point of view which befits a Christian. We must take our stand upon hope, and boldly face the fact that, whether we like it or no, we are people of the twentieth century, with all which that wild century has meant and still may mean. We cannot go back, so we may as well go on, and go on with all the confidence which we can muster.

As we said before, there are two philosophies now in vogue which, in some degree, bind their adherents to a particular course of action. They are, as it were, definitely committed to a certain point of view. The philosophies of Marxism and Existentialism. Both are far more than a mere way of thinking; they are a way of life. If this be true of them, pagan creeds of a moment, surely it is a thousand times more true of the Christian religion? To-day none of us can escape the obligation to live our Faith if we profess it at all. If Existentialism and Marxism demand the gift of self from their respective followers; if they demand that they should perpetually pursue an ideal and perpetually exercise their power of initiative and choice: surely we Christians can give no less to God? We choose too: but we choose His will.

Now the choice of God's will, on every occasion and in every circumstance of life, demands the very real exercise of our own. It is, as in the case of those two other philosophies, far more than an intellectual acknowledgment of the rightness of such and such a system: it is the definite acknowledgment of the obligation to live according to it. The very core of the principle of all three is that one should 'engage' oneself. Communism engages one for the supposed good of the mass: Existentialism engages one for the good of the individual, i.e. for self: Christianity engages one for the glory of God and the eternal happiness and welfare of all mankind, to be achieved by the personal salvation of each individual.

Incidentally it is a fact that, although they would only hate them the more, yet both the Marxist and the Existentialist would probably understand the actual priest, religious, or lay-apostle, better than they would understand the all-too-general type of Christian who professes his religion, goes to church on Sunday, has his children baptized, sends them if convenient to Catholic schools, and thereafter lives as do other men, whether they have a religion or not.

With regard to priests and religious, whatever our wrongheadedness and whatever our limitations in their eyes, we are at least 'engaged' in the sense in which they feel themselves to be. Although for them our religion may be absurd, a delusive, even a wicked religion, mixed up with capitalism on the one hand and with superstition and childish credulity on the other, yet we too have turned it into a way of life which they can comprehend. In that sense we fight them on a level; we are genuine adversaries, as staunchly opposed to their remedies for the problems of existence as they are to ours.

Let us make no mistake about it. If this last war ever fully develops, it is we who will have to bear the brunt of it this time. Indeed behind the Iron Curtain it is the priests and the religious who are already bearing it. It has only to spread a little further to the West for us to be equally involved. A spiritual war is a war with no quarter for those who profess the things of the spirit. We, who are sometimes accused of being escapists by those who have to grapple with a more commercial, more domestic form of life, will not be found to have chosen the way of escape should those days come.

In the meantime do not let us forget that it will be on the way in which we have lived now, in our still comparatively peaceful country, that will depend how we shall live then, how we shall fight for God. If we have turned away from the hard things, if we have not learned to make a stand for our religion and our principles, how can we expect to rise for the great occasion, the great opportunity, if it ever comes?

In the earlier stages of the spiritual life we have to overcome our will very often, to bend it consciously and painfully to accept the will of God. Let us take for a moment the example of the saints in order to see what we ourselves have to try and achieve. Their strong will has often, it is true, to be used in opposition to the will of creatures. Nothing can be more inflexible and adamantine than the will of a saint against evil. Yet when it comes to the will of God, there is not even one second's opposition. It is this strange combination of strength and pliability which is one of the secrets of the saints.

If we too are to use our liberty; if we are to set out to choose and to adopt the course we determine to follow; if we are to 'engage' ourselves actively with existence and not merely to drift with the tide; how are we to unite this freedom and will of ours with the will of God? The answer is simple: only by the grace of God Himself. And the way to obtain grace is to pray for it.

Looking back on life, even when we are still young, we often see that we made a mistake years ago—usually over something which we then ardently wanted. In other words, we made a mistake over just some such choice as we have been speaking of. How then are we to ensure that all our choices will not be similar mistakes? When we are told to live boldly, to give ourselves generously, we perhaps hesitate a little. Is it not wiser, safer, less painful, to drift with the tide of events: to see what to-morrow will bring with it, to wait and watch for a lead? But the lead is always there. The lead is the will of God by means of the things of God. We cannot get at the things of God by means of material devices.

We ourselves, it is true, are not capable of knowing for certain what is best and happiest for us, even up to the end of our life on earth. With our short-sighted vision we cannot even be assured of making a right deci-sion for as much as the duration of time. We realize that: and yet we still do not realize where it is that we go wrong in our prayer. We cannot understand why God does not grant all our requests: requests which will inevitably affect not only our time but our eternity. We see only the little bit of life which surrounds us at the moment: we know our yesterdays but not our to-morrows.

We admit of course theoretically that God knows not only our whole time but our whole eternity. But what is even more important is that He knows not only *our* eternity but His own: eternity itself. That is where in practice, and under the stress of our desires, we some-times misunderstand the use of prayer, and misunder-stand the manner of the union of our will with the will of God. We cannot imagine, in any one particular case, that what we want could really be contrary to His will. We ask ourselves why it should be. It is a good thing in itself; it is for our happiness, we are sure, because we know that we shall be so unhappy if we do not get it. God wants us to be happy—of course He does—then why should He not give us what we are asking of Him?

The answer is that indeed we do not know why—but that in His merciful foreknowledge, He does. Later on, even in this life, we too may see why we were refused.

We think in our distress that God is unmindful of us, that He is not 'answering', and we quote texts about sparrows in a bewildered manner. But He *is* answering, only, as the small boy protested to his mother when, with the strange density characteristic of some grown-ups, she was trying to console him for a seemingly unnoticed request, "only the answer was 'No'."

So often the answer is that merciful 'No', which understands our needs and our happiness so much better than we do. Could we force a 'Yes' to that same prayer, and then review it after the lapse of, say, twenty years, how often we ourselves should be the first to cry out that we had been wrong, wrong, wrong! We should wish over and over again that God had given us the answer which we are now refusing to accept, and feeling so sore because our folly is being denied us.

Sometimes it even seems as if we could force God's hand. We have our free-will, and if we push, and insist, and urge—if not actually culpably against, at all events blind to the will of God—we may succeed in getting our own way. We shall then of course proceed to call it His. God does not force. His will is absolute, yet, in our own affairs, it is part of that very Will that the play of our freedom which He never takes from us, may seem to obstruct His plan. We will not listen? We will not take 'No'? Very well then, we take 'Yes'. But it is we who take it and not God who gives it. It is never a good 'Yes' for us.

That does not mean that we should not pray. "Ask and ye shall receive." Needs, graces, miracles, all come to us and to others through supplication. But the prayer, particularly when it is a case of our own affairs, is humble, gentle; it is never a pushing of our personal will. It is a seeking to know the will of God; an appeal to God to show us what He wants and what is best, and for grace to bear it if it means pain for us. And the answer when it comes, and whatever it may be, will be courageously accepted.

It is not so much a hard and fast prayer to God to do so and so; to wrench matters to such an issue; to override this or that; as a humble and loving "Show us what You want, dear God overrule everything for Your glory; let events, which seem to us so difficult and hard, move according to Your plan and Your desire, and they will move as we desire also. In Your mercy, do not let us obstruct You by our folly and our blindness."

Let us pray that we may have the grace to leave God's wisdom to act for us, to arrange things for His glory and for our ultimate joy. Let our prayer be a desperate appeal to God—the more desperate, the more violent our human longing—not to let us obstruct His will. But let it never be an appeal to Him to grant us our own way at the cost of His.

CHAPTER XXII

IN THE DAYS OF THE
ANCHORESSES

THE door of the tiny hot-cupboard had stuck; there was no doubt of it; and the trouble was that I was inside. The key locked and unlocked perfectly from the corridor, there was no doubt of that either, for it was always kept locked except on the rare occasions when something was put in there to dry; but unfortunately I had brought the key in with me and absent-mindedly turned it, and nothing would induce it to turn back. The small window was obviously no use as an exit, indeed scarcely any use even for air, and looked out only over a sun-baked, slanting roof.

It was a burning hot August day, and the tank for once was exceedingly hot. Since I could not make anyone hear, I began instead to say the rosary—for the Holy Souls. After what seemed to be hours, there was a faint footfall in the passage, and "Sister!" I cried, my mouth close to the crack of the door. By the grace of God it was the voice of Sister Imelda which answered.

"Who is it? Where is it? What is it?"

I could not see her expression, but I gathered from the tone of voice that she thought she was being addressed by a spirit from beyond. I half expected her to say "Avaunt" next.

"Who art thou?" she demanded, instinctively adopting the language usually considered the most suitable for conversing with ghosts.

"Me!" I replied emphatically, only too conscious of the flesh.

"You?"

"Yes."

"How did you get there?"

"The usual way."

"Why don't you come out?"

"Try the door and you'll know," I was almost beyond the superfluities of polite conversation. There was a pause filled by fumbling, during which I continued to drip gently on to the floor.

"Pass the key under the door and I will unlock it from this side."

"Won't come out."

"Dear, dear!" Pause. "I'll go and get some tools. Sure you are not hurt? Lint? Bandages? Plaster?"

"How do you propose to plaster me? Could you get me *out* do you think?"

"Of course I can. Aren't you very tired? How long have you been there? *Do* sit down." Her voice was the voice of a kind hostess at a tea-party. There was only the tank to sit upon, and the tank was now unmistakably boiling. I could positively hear it singing, like a kettle.

"Get the tools, Sister dear; be an angel and get that door open somehow."

There was a prolonged silence while I sat upon the floor and mused—mostly upon the Holy Souls. Presently there was the sound of returning footsteps followed by discreet whispering.

"Are you still there?" enquired a low voice through the crack.

"I am sorry to say I am."

"Not hungry?"

Carmelites are not in the habit of eating between meals and I said so. My voice, I fancied, sounded a little dry—the effect, I hoped, of the unaccustomed heat, and not of anything worse.

"I wish," said Sister Imelda anxiously to someone invisible, "that we could pass her through a biscuit."

"Glass of water would be better," replied the unmistakable voice of Sister Elizabeth, "it must be boiling in there with that tank. Can't we get her out?"

"You couldn't get some water out of the tank, could you?" enquired Sister Imelda, instantly putting the two ideas together.

"I would rather get out myself if you don't mind. Did you bring any tools?"

"Lots," said Sister Elizabeth. I oozed gratitude from every pore.

It took half an hour or more, and the jamb had to be taken off but, supported by encouraging remarks, they managed it in the end. Sister Imelda led me forth in triumph, which changed to something very like horror as she stared at me.

"I've never seen you that colour before," she said at last in an awed whisper.

"I've never *been* that colour before," I assured her.

"Not a moment too soon," said Sister Elizabeth cheerfully, "you're purple."

"The next stage is black," Sister Imelda confided to us, and led me downstairs, guided by her unerring bump for appropriateness, into the kitchen. It seemed to me, deliciously, the most cool and airy place which I had ever been in. I sat upon a stool while Sister Elizabeth stood about solicitously, still carrying the tools.

"Would you believe it, she has been a prisoner in the hot cupboard," explained Sister Imelda to the First-in-the-Kitchen, who appeared, after one glance at my countenance, to have no difficulty in believing anything, and said "Tch—tch—tch——" several times.

"A *gôdet* of cold water," advised Sister Elizabeth, "and then fresh air."

"Won't she catch cold?" As a matter of fact there was nothing I more ardently desired to catch at the moment.

"You have had a very wonderful experience," said Sister Imelda soberly as we arrived at her carpentering shed a few moments later. She, also, had insisted upon a dose of fresh air, and as the only alternative appeared to be a biscuit, which she still continued to offer me vaguely at intervals, I suggested her workshop by way of diversion. If I had sat upon the equator itself I could not have caused more consternation; Sister Elizabeth kept watching me in a way which I found disconcerting. I suppose that seeing a person slowly turning every shade like a chameleon is rather absorbing, but my own feeling was that the sooner we all forgot about it the better. In spite of Sister Imelda's adjective 'wonderful', I had a little difficulty in regarding an hour or two in the hot cupboard as the culminating experience of my life.

"Let me look at the designs for your next Christmas cards," I suggested.

"Wonderful! " she repeated, opening a drawer and laying out the sketches one by one on the table. "Don't you see?—— Now you *really* know what it feels like to be an anchoress! "

"Anchoress! " I put down the sketch I had picked up. Why on earth had that not struck me at the actual moment, as it certainly would have struck her? Ancress —I prefer the older word—and what had I done with the brief interlude? Nothing, absolutely nothing, except to say a few rosaries for the Holy Souls and drip gently on to everything I met. Sister Imelda was right; she would never have missed the opportunity of a lifetime like that.

"You know, that is our real vocation, and now you have lived it if only for a couple of hours. Shut in both ways: one tiny window on to the world: everything complete and perfect." But *had* I lived it? That was the point.

"They didn't boil their anchoresses anyway," said Sister Elizabeth practically.

"No, they didn't boil them but . . ."

"Yes, yes," I put in hastily, "we know all about those buts. It was not very clean, or hygienic, or anything of that sort, but the spiritual part, as you say, was wonderful."

"It is our inheritance," said Sister Imelda gently.

I picked up the sketch and looked at it again. Of course: that was it: that was what *Sponsa Christi* was aiming at all the time. The continuity of it. The enclosed contemplatives as the direct descendants of the consecrated virgins of the earliest Christian days.

In England, the *Ancren Riwle*, a semi-Saxon tract, dates back to the thirteenth century.[1] The probable author was Bishop Richard Poore, who held the See of Salisbury from 1217-1229, and was then transferred to Durham, and finally died at his birthplace, Tarrent in Dorsetshire, in 1237. It is thought that he wrote the Rule for some anchoresses, or nuns, who lived at his old home, Tarrent, on the river Stour.

The life of a recluse was not necessarily completely solitary. In this particular case there appear to have been as many as three living together in one anchorhold, although separately, each having her rooms apart, something in the manner of the Carthusian Order. This was so also with regard to the anchorage, the remains of which

[1] A translation of this was made in about 1853 by James Morton for the Camden Society.

can still be seen in the churchyard of St. George's chapel at Shrewsbury.

The more usual form of life for these recluses, however, was a single cell, or sometimes two rooms, built against the wall of a church, with a small window looking directly on to the sanctuary and within sight of the high altar and the Blessed Sacrament. Such solitaries were not necessarily walled-up, although the practice was fairly common.

"Present-day contemplative nuns—*moniales*—are, after all, their direct descendants," said Sister Imelda smiling happily at the thought. "Read their old Rule and *you will notice how all their customs have come down to us.* The directions for the prayers on getting up in the morning; the keeping of silence from Compline to the *Pretiosa* of Prime; the saying of the Divine Office; the rules for the shutter of their window on to the world, with a grille, and a black curtain, precisely like ours to-day. All the rules for eating, fasting, and for the 'out-sisters', as he calls them, are exactly the same as our own. Ancresses were never to be idle, but continually work, or say the office, or read, or 'be at beads'. Isn't that exactly what *Sponsa Christi* insists upon now? Work, prayer, the solemn obligation of reciting the Divine Office 'in the name of the Church'? And the one beast they might keep—birds aren't beasts, of course,"— Sister Imelda was taking no risks—"was the domestic cat."

At the word cat Anthony raised his head and surveyed us knowingly. He was pleased, no doubt, to have his ancestry discussed and authenticated as dating back to the thirteenth century; but, after all, Pekin was considerably older than that. "Quite" he said condescendingly, and went to sleep again.

"The strange coincidence is that they said the same

things about them then that they say about us now," remarked Sister Imelda. "You can see that by the Introduction to the Rule, and the translator, even a hundred years ago, remarks that the life is 'unlike any that the modern world knows'."

"The life," said I sententiously, "will always be unlike any that the modern world knows, however much you try to bring it up to date, for the simple reason that it is not the *modern* world that it is unlike but the world itself. The spirit of the world in those days was as opposed to the spirit of the anchoresses as the spirit of the world now is opposed to the spirit of the contemplative vocation, and that is the truth about it in a nutshell."

"Fundamental opposition," said Sister Imelda briskly and cheerfully; indeed she seemed rather pleased about it; "and there is one comfort, in many ways the things they said about them then, were even worse than anything they say about us now."

"Shall we look at some more Christmas cards," I suggested hastily. I was not taking any risks either, for after all the novice was present. Sister Elizabeth smiled.

"I have often wondered, now you mention it," she remarked, in her pleasant dreamy voice, "whether, if we had lived in those days, when it came to wanting to go on a pilgrimage to Canterbury, our mothers might not have said that they would rather we waited until we were a little older."

Sister Imelda and I sank together into an aghast silence.

"I only wondered," murmured the novice meekly.

In the case of the ancresses there was evidently a good deal of carping at the habit they wore then, just as there is at ours nowadays, because the good Bishop Poore warns his nuns not to worry if any ignorant person should ask them of what Order they are, "as you tell me some do, who strain at the gnat and swallow the fly"; or again, "whether white or black, as foolish people ask you, who think that Order consists in the kirtle or the cowl; God knoweth nevertheless, they may well wear both, not, however as to clothes, but as God's Bride singeth of herself 'I am black and yet white', dark outwardly and bright within. In this manner answer ye anyone who asks you concerning your Order, and—whether white or black— say that ye are both through the grace of God. . . . To keep himself pure and unspotted from the world, herein is religion, and not in the wide hood—nor in the black, nor in the white, nor in the grey cowl".

Even the vows are the same then as now, except that we have added a further vow of Poverty. "No anchoress, by my advice, shall make profession, that is, *vow* to keep anything as commanded, except three things, that is obedience, chastity, and constancy as to her abode." These are to be invariable, and then he goes on to speak of many things which may be rightly and reasonably varied by the Rule.

All that was seven hundred years ago, and here we are, contemplative nuns the world over, still doing the same and bearing the same to-day.

"But charity or love, and meekness and patience, truthfulness, and keeping the ten old commandments, confession and penitence, these and such others, some of which are of the old law, some of the new, are not of man's invention, nor a rule established by man, but they are the commandments of God, and therefore every man is bound and obliged to keep them, and ye most of all; for they govern the heart. . . ."

"Govern the heart," I said out loud, and Sister Imelda asked me what I was thinking about.

"I was only thinking that even if we are not walled up any longer, even if perhaps we have necessarily to come more in contact with the world, if there is less solitude and silence. . . ."

"But there isn't!" cried Sister Imelda flatly. "Don't trouble yourself about that—on the contrary, it is the other way round."

Sister Elizabeth stared at her in astonishment. "My!" she exclaimed suitably.

"Oh, yes: anchoresses *were* solitary and they *were* silent, but it was in the heart that they carried their solitude and their silence. That's what her old bishop," she pointed at me, "meant by his 'they govern the heart'. Unless all those things come to us from God, from the soul inside ourselves, they are of no more use than any other set of rules might be—ration books, or poultry feeding stuff regulations, which people spend their time trying to break. It is not the bit of paper and the printing on it, nor, for the matter of that, the cursory reading of it every day; it is what is in the mind and in the heart —the *love* of it. The anchoresses had their window on to the world just as we have ours: more than we have, because theirs were straight on to the world, they could see the background as well as the visitor, and, thank God, we can't, not even if it is someone to whom we are obliged to open the shutter. Oh, no, we have gone forwards since then, not backward —the state of religion as a whole, I mean. Make no mistakes about it, the things of God increase—improve—or they falter and wither away altogether." Sister Imelda folded her two little hands on the table in front of her and regarded me earnestly, almost beseechingly.

"We haven't withered away and died," she said, "not even in Protestant, pagan England, not even surrounded by Communism, and Existentialism, and Psychiatry, and all the modern misery. . . ." She stopped.

"No," I said slowly, "we haven't done that."

Sister Elizabeth almost threw the sketch she had been looking at down upon the table, and her voice had an edge on it which I had never heard before.

"And we shan't!" she said. "We shan't!"

Sister Imelda gave a little sigh and smiled at her. I found myself smiling too.

"We pin our faith to God," said I, "and to the rising generation."

CHAPTER XXIII

YOUTH

CAMILLA'S voice sounded thoroughly disgruntled. "Is that you?" she enquired politely but without enthusiasm.

"It is," I admitted. "What is the matter?"

"Everything is the matter," said Camilla, sighing heavily through the grille. I waited patiently. Presently the voice began again. "I am sick to death of doing everything to-day and then beginning to do it all over again to-morrow. Why can't things *stay* done when you've done them?"

"Now that," I agreed appreciatively, "is one of the most interesting problems in life. What a brain you have, Camilla! Wars, and bills, and amateur piano-playing—once they are over and finished, why can't they stay finished? But they can't; just as we are thanking God, they always begin again. Which particular recurring tragedy is yours at the moment?"

"All my life is a recurring tragedy," said Camilla with an unmistakable sniff, whether of tears or contempt I could not tell since the grille between us was firmly closed in its usual heartless way. "Talking of pianos, what do you think that new celebrity said to me the other day when we were introduced at a party? *You* know, the latest pianist." I did not know, needless to say, but Camilla was beyond trifles of that sort. "He said: 'Do you play the violin?' I shook my head, 'Do you sing?' I shook it again. 'Do this—?' He ran his fingers up

220

and down imaginary keys. I shook it once more. 'Thank God! ' he said, and was so relieved he never spoke again the whole evening."

"I sympathize," I murmured soothingly, without however specifying with whom. Suddenly Camilla gave it up.

"I am sorry to be so tiresome," she said in her ordinary voice. "The fact is, it is just everything! I can stand weeks and weeks of monotony as a rule, with something pleasant round the corner; but it's this months and months of monotony with nothing pleasant in sight anywhere, and not even one corner. . . . I just can't bear it any longer."

"So that," I said to myself, "is how the young in the world—some of them anyway—are feeling."

It is, of course, a little inherent in feminine nature, that subconscious sensation of being a drudge. And the further away a woman gets from it mentally, the more she probably resents any hint of it. In the old days, when she really was a drudge, I do not suppose she very much minded.

"Heaven-in-the-end is the answer to it all, Camilla, you'll find that out one day."

"I dare say," she agreed politely, "but meanwhile I've got to go on living on earth until I do. Look here. . . ." We settled down at last to the real trouble, which from the first had obviously been the motive of the visit.

As I walked away from the parlour half an hour later, I realized more than ever that human nature does not change. Camilla was only feeling as so many of us had felt twenty years earlier, and as so many would feel twenty years on.

What, I asked myself, in the cause of the strange restlessness of youth: of that half-pain, half-joy of the years of the spring of life? Every generation in turn senses it, every generation in turn passes away and out of it, yet no one has ever told us precisely where the trouble lies, nor where the remedy. Looking back, it seems that we just grew out of it. If indeed we ever did. It is a long road from youth to middle-age.

One thing seems clear: in ordinary, daily life, the old should never try to *legislate* for the young. Let them listen, sympathize, advise if necessary, and leave it at that. The two points of view are too far apart. They have worn out the sharpness of their emotions. How sometimes it can hurt, that soothing and entirely detached, " Don't worry. . . ." as if one were a fractious child, and as if anyone would worry who could help it. After all, one cannot mend a broken heart by telling a person not to mind: one can only make the pain of the break sharper. And broken hearts are very real things even in these advanced and emancipated days.

" Soon mended! " say the old, smiling and shrugging their shoulders. But not always so very soon, and not always in the end. And very rarely, in any case, without the loss of ideals which could ill be spared.

The old have balance—wisdom: they can judge—suggest: but when it comes to acting for the young, they forget how bitter is grief at that age: how passionate is joy: how eternal seems disappointment. When people have grown old they have learned, indeed, that nothing lasts; but when we are young, it seems to us, on the contrary, that things will never end. Let us be kind to youth, learn how to bear with its impetuosities, its pain, its gallant hope.

It is easy to wish that youth were more restrained, less turbulent; but, apart from the fact that it almost invariably cannot, it would not even be right for youth to feel like middle-age. It is a bad thing actually when the young take habitually to not worrying, to letting things

slide. That is the corrective to the fussiness of old age,
but it should not be applied before the time. If age
does not take things a little more easily, it is true that it
is apt to accentuate in the opposite direction and to become unbearably particular; but if youth takes things
too easily at the beginning, it only becomes increasingly
careless and frivolous. In age that slight slackening, that
letting things pass, comes from tolerance, wisdom, understanding; in youth it could not come from such developed
virtues, which normally are only acquired with the years.

Youth reacts warmly, ardently, to life and should do
so. The reason *is*—quite simply—its youth. Take anything young: a kitten so earnestly chasing its tail: a
puppy joyously chewing up its first boot. No use to tell
them that tails only lead one round and round in the
same direction until one is giddy, and that shoe-polish
makes one sick. They, in company with their young
masters and mistresses, are meeting everything for the
first time — religion — love — rabbits — friendship —
mice—careers—and finding out about things in general.
Some will do it almost recklessly, flinging themselves at
experience, gobbling up emotions; others more cauti-
ously, with a tentative foot set on the untried path. But
the reactions are bound to be there in either case. Their
first, unique reactions to life. To tell youth not to worry
is to tell youth not to live.

The trouble is that there is a certain temperament
which is inclined, in any case, to follow such advice—
which has, in fact, already given itself similar advice—
and so will be encouraged to stand back and allow events
to flow past, watching opportunity slip by on the current,
half envious, half scornful, of the experiences, the sur-
prises, the enchanting discoveries which are youth's
happy prerogative.

Experience at second hand is not altogether a good

thing, even at its best. In our later years it may be sufficient to watch, to study, to take the faintly aloof view
of maturity. But it is well to have touched life, and been
touched by it, first. Some people even manage, and may
God be thanked for it, to go on living, fully, happily, with
all their pristine enthusiasm, tempered no doubt by the
knowledge and the kindliness of long experience, up to
the very end.

Let age deal wisely and understandingly with youth—
with the *state* of youth, that is. It is a very important
state, not only for those who enjoy it but for the world at
large. Youth does not last just for its few brief years and
perish: most of us, for all our lives, are what it has made
us.

Not to legislate too rigidly for youth, however, does not
mean not to give help and encouragement when it is
needed. One can make mistakes almost as badly in that
direction as in the other. "Without backing and without lead" was the bitter expression used by a young girl
honestly trying to make something of life against an
enveloping atmosphere of complete indifference. The
pain of earth is there for all of us at times, but at least
we need not make the pain any worse for those with
whom we live.

It is hard enough to bear the disappointments, the
business failures perhaps, the friendships which go
wrong, the death of those whom we had thought indispensable to our happiness, the frustrated ambitions of
our early years which we had so confidently counted on
achieving. Even the very gifts which some may feel that
God has given them may yet have missed their mark because the circumstances were never quite right for their
development. There is the loneliness for others of the in-
between years, when the young people seem to have
grown up and forgotten, and the old ones have gone to

God; or the greater loneliness of those for ever separated from their families by the confusion and misery of war. And there is that last, strange disillusionment of the achieved ambition which when tasted is found, after all, to have no taste.

Even on a much broader basis, there is the sadness of the realization of national and political disaster, of the passing of the days of culture and high achievement. "The lights are going out all over Europe," said Sir Edward Grey in the August days of 1914, "and they will never be relit in our time." And that brings us to the heart of the inescapable suffering of existence, and its meaning for each individual.

It is clear how the Marxist regards it: clear too what the Existentialist makes of it, and how the Pagan reacts to the inevitable. But what have we Christians to do with it, that is the point for us? It is a good thing to know those other ways of thinking, precisely in order that we may avoid their blind mistakes, their misunderstanding of life, their tragic misapprehension of death. There are many ways of dealing with day to day troubles and sorrows: ways of grappling with ourselves and with our circumstances: of smiling our way through difficulties and laughing quite genuinely at mishaps. But none of these go to the root of the problem.

For a Christian, suffering is always God's action upon the soul. That is the immense difference between our view of it and the view of the rest of the world. There is no blind chance involved. Sometimes, it is true, we may by our folly or by our ignorance have brought it upon ourselves; in that case God will use it to show us our mistake and to help us retrieve it, for, even so, it could not have happened without His knowledge and His permission. Sometimes, again, others may have brought it upon us, and then God will know how to watch over us

P

and to turn it to our ultimate spiritual advantage; we need never be afraid that He will not, if only we know how to trust Him, how to bear the pain of it in the meantime. Or, last of all, it may be God's direct intention for us, His way of beginning our purification even here on earth. As we grow more fully into the spiritual life, we come to realize better the benefit of this direct action and, with comprehension, the suffering of it grows less.

There is many a trial which would be almost unbearable if we attributed it solely to the malice of others, or to mere 'bad luck' which had chanced to overtake us: but which assumes an altogether different appearance, and produces an altogether different effect, when we learn to attribute it to its real source—the love of God for us.

And so, in a contrary sense, just because we believe that all pain is over-ruled by God, let us take and enjoy whole-heartedly the periods of happiness which so often come to us. Even in this century of world-suffering there are still compensations, still sunlit moments when we can forget everything except the beautiful earth on which we live and the goodness of God who made it, and set us in it for His glory. There is a right way of taking these moments just as surely as there is a right way of taking suffering, for both come equally from God, and both leave an indelible mark upon the soul. When, in our spiritual life, we have some such sunny space of time, let us rest in it and be content to relax. Do not let us try to think it out; to ask questions; to wonder why we did not feel like this last week, and whether we shall still be feeling like it the day after to-morrow. Do not let us calculate God's graces, classify them, and try to draw maps of them for our future reference.

Let us *live* our joy as we have had to live our sorrow. And when it is over, as over it will be sooner or later, so long as we are on this earth, let us go gallantly back to our purgative suffering, remembering that that too is only a part of the whole.

There is an Italian railway which runs down the coast by Genoa to Rome and, as the train goes, it slips continually in and out of little black tunnels, and in and out of little splashes of golden sunlight, wet with the spray of waves which beat against the rocks below. It has always seemed to me that life is very much the same.

To get at the real value and meaning of our suffering in Time, we have to see it in relation to our joy in Eternity. We have also to remember our personal need of purgation from sin. St. Augustine tells us that the punishment of purgatory is temporary and will cease, at the very latest, with the Last Judgment. "But", he goes on, and this is the solution of our problem if we care to take it as such, "temporary punishments are suffered by some in this life only, by others after death, by others both now and then; but all of them before the last, strictest judgment."[1]

What further answer do we need? What further consolation?

"No, we do not play the coward, though the outward part of our nature is being worn down, our inner life is refreshed from day to day. This light and momentary affliction brings with it a reward multiplied every way, loading us with everlasting glory; if only we will fix our eyes on what is unseen, not on what we can see. What we can see lasts but for a moment; what is unseen is eternal."[2]

[1] *De Civ. Dei, lib. XXI, cap. xiii & xvi.*
[2] The Epistle of St. Paul to the Corinthians, translated by Ronald Knox, iv, 16-18.

CHAPTER XXIV

HEARTBREAK HOUSE

THE suffering of the spiritual life is as different from the suffering of the world as two things called by the same name can well be. It differs in its surroundings, that is to say in the place in which it attacks us, in the faculties and emotions which it brings into play, and most of all in the effects which it leaves behind in us. The only thing which the two seem to have in common is the fact of the suffering itself.

This does not mean that the ordinary suffering of life cannot also be a spiritual suffering; it can; but it will always be clear, at all events to those who are trying to live a spiritual life, whether in the world or out of it, which part is the human and which the spiritual. For the crux of the matter lies in the will. The moment the will comes into play and tries to join the human pain to the will of God the pain itself becomes spiritualized, at all events in part. The ordinary suffering of life—the ravages of disease, disappointment, failure, death—as borne by a pagan is one thing; the ordinary suffering of life as perceived and borne by a Christian is quite another. Yet the actual source of the suffering may be the same in both cases: it is the reaction to it, the view taken of it, which either makes of it a spiritual thing or leaves it completely earthly.

Speaking very generally one could perhaps say that there are three forms which human suffering may take. The suffering of life suffered without the thought of

God: the suffering of life joined to the thought of God: purely spiritual suffering arising, in the main, from the longing desire of the soul to unite itself to God, and its consciousness of its utter unworthiness and incapacity. This particular type of spiritual suffering is almost entirely passive and the effect is definitely purgative. It burns. If we suffer it willingly, and rightly, giving the co-operation of our acceptance of it, it does its work unaided. The only thing necessary to set its action free in the soul, one might perhaps say, is our initial consent. Such suffering the saints know.

For the rest of us, it is safer, when assessing what can rightly be termed spiritual suffering, to make sure that it has, however interior its *effects* may be, some solid, exterior source. Otherwise, however good our intentions, we may become lost in the mazes of pure imagination and self-pity. All the normal events and vicissitudes of life, as we said before, such as loss of money and position, illness, thwarted affections, insuccess in any ambition, uncongenial surroundings, the misunderstanding of those forming part of our environment, and so on, may cause immense interior suffering, with immense purgative power, but the suffering is normal, *genuine*.

The range and scope of such human pain is indeed so wide that it is almost impossible to set limits to it, but there are nevertheless two qualities which, if it is to be counted as in any degree spiritual suffering, should characterize it: it is borne without self-pity and it does not induce egoism. The people enduring it may speak of it if needs be, since in many cases the calamity is visible to all, but they will not very willingly, nor to very many, speak of their own reactions to it. In this it can easily be distinguished from all the forms of neurosis or egocentricity which seek to mask themselves as spirituality.

We in modern days, however, tend perhaps more to

extroversion than to introversion as a generation, apart from definitely psychological sufferers. Take, for instance, the attitude of those three ancient kings who sought the even greater King whose star they had seen in the East. It was the King Himself whom they were genuinely looking for and, once found, they never questioned his surroundings, unlikely as these were.

So often with us, on the contrary, it is the surroundings of a thing upon which we unconsciously concentrate— the glamour, the 'atmosphere' of our idea or of our hero. Whoever can surround himself with those, can play the monarch to his own little circle, or sometimes even to the world, for a short decade or two. The other King was born in a stable and crucified upon a lonely hill. And there, in some sort of general analogy, is to be found the difference between the fanciful spiritual suffering of the egoist and dreamer, and the real spiritual suffering of the seeker after Christ: the studied and elaborate *mise en scène* of the one and the unassuming loneliness of the other.

I spoke one day of these things to Sister Imelda. I had often wondered what place, what value, she had given to suffering in her apparently sunny life. I was not sufficiently foolish to suppose that she had managed, either by design or inadvertently, to evade it, however successfully she might try to convince us to the contrary by her radiant and constant joyousness.

"Suffering?" she said with a smile. "You mean Heartbreak House; that is what I always call it to myself. It is the only way to God."

It was a golden day at the end of summer; soon the misty dawns and early twilights of autumn would be upon us. But as yet every leaf still hung in unshaded green upon its bough; no streak of yellow or red betrayed the nearness of the waiting winds of winter.

"Heartbreak House," I repeated slowly, "a pretty name. I did not know you had ever been there."

"Oh, yes," she said, and said no more.

"Would you tell me a little about it?"

"Why, yes, in general. But it will be no more than you know. Everyone who wants to turn into a real person, and not just remain a fancy figure all through life, has to pass that way."

"A fancy figure?"

She looked at me with her deep blue eyes. "Now don't pretend that you don't know what I mean by a fancy figure of a person," she said reprovingly.

"Well—yes—I suppose I do," I admitted.

"It is a strange place, because we go in at one door, but we leave it, if ever we do leave it, by another; and the door we leave it by is the Will of God just as surely as the door we enter it by is our own will. It was Adam and Eve who first lived in Heartbreak House, and it was they, never God, who made the door into it. You will find Heartbreak House in ordinary life, and Heartbreak House in the spiritual life, but the way into both is always by the will—either by not getting what we want, or else by very definitely getting what we don't want."

"Are they not one and the same?"

"Not in the least. Getting what we don't want, well, that is something to put up with, but it can usually be done, however hard it is. But not getting what we wanted so badly—ah, there is the rub: that is a thousand times worse. It is not having to put up with, but it is having to do without, which is the real hardship of life."

"I believe you are right," I said, and looked at a sky turned pale by contrast with the glory of the sun, and the crimson and green of the orchard trees.

"Heartbreak House in the spiritual life is just as real as it is in ordinary life. It is still not getting what we want. We want to be saints and we aren't. We want to reach sanctity quickly in our own particular way and we can't. We dream, and we complain, and we excuse ourselves, and we blame others for it, and all the time we are trying to walk out of Heartbreak House by the door we came in at."

"Go on."

"I think that in this sort of suffering it is never the surroundings which form the pain itself. Either in the world, or with us in here, they are only the framework. The suffering itself is individual, held within that frame, but the frame is not it. Circumstances, surroundings, you see they are all exterior, general, common to men as a whole: the real thing begins—we ourselves begin—where they end."

I thought of the door into Heartbreak House and the door out of it; and yet, so often, long before we enter, we have discovered what we genuinely believe to be our true vocation, and that means the vocation to which God calls us. What then are we doing in Heartbreak House at all? So many never even find their real vocation in life; they drift, they wander, they stumble into their way of living, never knowing what they have missed. But those who have once heard the authentic call, no matter to what form of life, can never forget it. For a vocation is never to an isolated act, it is to a way of living; it is continuous, it stretches into the future, its vistas open endlessly before us, and in that is its greatest joy. It is not something we are going to do to-morrow, it is something we are doing for all time. We may not follow the call: through sloth, through fear, through lack of stability: but we have had our moment: that moment when we knew, past doubting, knew with a singing happiness, that this was what we could do—could be—were born to do and be.

"Does anyone ever guess,
When the watch ticking over his heart,
Marks his loveliest hour?

.   .   .   .   .   .

What eyes for a vision!
What hearts for a Resurrection!
What lives there are,
Sharp like spears forfending
Foes that threaten a spark,
Which will still be burning
After the last star."

It is the moment when we know that, for us, the world is well lost for love. The immediate object of love may be varied a thousand times, but love itself is always a part of God. And our true vocation, when we have found it, is always followed for love alone; that is how we know that it is true. No gain, no greed, no applause, no recognition, come into it anywhere: we feed our little spark and live by its glow, simply because we are ourselves, and no one else, and it is the dearest part of that self.

When it is the direct following of Christ which is our vocation, life loses all its complications and comes to mean one thing only to us—His will. In so far as it is possible to frail and imperfect creatures, we will with the will of God, perhaps it were better to say that the gift of the free-will has been made with so much love that although, except in the case of the saints, much human imperfection still clings to it, yet that love carries us always to prefer the plan of God to our own.

The difference may be seen at a glance. There are many excellent plans made for the glory of God and the good of others: they are worked for, prayed for, God is asked to bless them, and does bless them. But they

remain the plans of those who made them—under God.
These other plans in which we find ourselves involved
when we have made the shy gift of our will to Him, are
not our plans at all. They are His work alone and we
only pray that we may not spoil them.

Our recurring human frailty makes no difference to
this ultimate vocation. When we feel, as indeed we all
do at times, that we cannot love, we cannot even dimly
care, we cannot do anything: then, having learnt to will
with God's will which He has lent to us, let us ask also
to love with His love, having none of our own: not His
love with which to comfort our cold selves: not the return of our own natural love with which to comfort
others: but the gift or the lending of His love with which
to love both Himself and all the world for His dear
sake.

And that is the door which leads out of Heartbreak
House. The house which Christ Himself, our brother,
entered for love of us, and the door which He first went
through, when for love of us He did the will of His
Father.

As the perfect composer-conductor draws his own
music out of an orchestra, so God draws our little part
in His creation out of us. The music, as we listen to it,
beats against us like an overmastering wind, carries us
up to heaven, makes us laugh with the joy of it; but all
the time, underneath, it is composed of the thousand
little threads of sound drawn from each instrument, mys-
terious, soft, pliable as silk.

If we will leave the movement and the rhythm of the
vast composition to Him, and watch only for the individual wave of the hand, the slight turning of the head in
our direction, which mean that it is our moment now,
that here we come in—while presently we shall fade
quietly out again and the violins will take up the *motif* in

our place—then, even on earth, this Heartbreak Earth, we shall know the enduring happiness of the true vocation found and followed. Like good musicians we shall forget everything—everyone—except our music, and Him who wrote it, marvellously, inexplicably, just for us.